INTIMATE ENCOUNTERS WITH GOD

Compiled by

Linda Evans Shepherd

and

Eva Marie Everson

HONOR HB BOOKS

Inspiration and Motivation for the Season of Life

An Imprint of Cook Communications Ministries • Colorado Springs, CO

07 06 05 04 03   10 9 8 7 6 5 4 3 2 1

Intimate Encounters with God
ISBN 1-56292-499-0
Copyright © 2003 by Right to the Heart
Published by Honor Books
An Imprint of Cook Communications Ministries
4050 Lee Vance View
Colorado Springs, CO 89018

Developed by Bordon Books

Foreword

Do you love friendly mail? Then you'll love *Intimate Encounters with God* because these life-letters (stories) have been written out of the powerful and tender exchanges between heaven and earth, between deity and humanity. The pages ahead overflow with encounters by members of the Advanced Writers and Speakers Association (AWSA), women who share their hearts to honor God and to bless you.

AWSA girls rock! Not as in rock n' roll (although I have heard their toes tapping), but as in Rock of Ages. And ages they are—as in "all," from the young to the ever so, well, uh, highly seasoned. While I am an AWSA participant and supporter, I don't have the availability to exchange e-mail transmissions with the "girls," because of my involvement with the Women of Faith tour most of the year; so I've been eavesdropping on them. What fun! I love mail. When I return home from my on-the-road lifestyle for a quick turnaround, I purposely take a few moments to catch up with my sisters by reading the backlog of e-mails that await me. It's like tuning in to a Christian reality show (It's about time!). Their zany humor and their expansive hearts refresh me. I am moved by the generous contributions they gladly make into each other's lives.

These are women who are solidly positioned in their faith. And while they are exceptional in their accomplishments, their struggles are commonplace. You may even recognize someone who has struggles just like yours. You are invited to eavesdrop with me on how God made Himself known to these women in a myriad of ways, amid life's distresses and delights.

Like you, these godly women understand first-hand the daily hardships of life, and they know what it is to have collided with unavoidable heartaches. But there's something else of which these Christian speakers and authors are intimately aware—encounters—God encounters: moments when God undeniably touches His children and leaves them changed, encouraged, and inspired.

I'm grateful for how creatively diverse the Lord is. Why, we might encounter His presence in the glistening of a dewdrop, a child's sparkling laughter, or a friend's compassionate touch. Or we might see Him in a narrow ray of hope while trudging through a shadow-immersed valley. One thing is for sure, if we seek him we will find him (that's not *my* promise— that's straight from the throne).

Admire with me these writers' sturdy courage and their winsome faith. Will they sound like Pollyannas? Far from it. These are in-the-trenches women, who have been sobered by great personal losses, stretched by ongoing struggles, and who have not just survived, but have grown through life's tough curriculum.

So I bid you to join my Christian girlfriends in their *Intimate Encounters with God*.

Patsy Clairmont
Author, Speaker, & AWSA Member

Contents

Nightlight

S u s a n   D u k e

Unto the upright there ariseth light in the darkness.

Psalm 112:4 KJV

I stepped outside to my back porch, feeling as lonely and empty as the midnight sky. No stars were in sight, and not even a sliver of light shone from the clandestine moon. I sat down in my old rocking chair, listening for a sign of life from the bleak stillness. But the only sound that emerged from my ebony sanctuary was that of the wooden rockers that groaned beneath my weight.

I'd somehow survived several months of losses—my precious eighteen-year-old son, my best friend, a dear family friend, and a twenty-one-year-old nephew, all within a very short period of time. I kept going physically, but, like the moon, my grieving heart was hidden behind clouds of sorrow and questions.

"Lord, I can't keep going through the motions of normalcy. My life will never be the same. I can't change that—and the darkness I'm feeling in my soul is because I know you can't change what's happened either. But you must realize I can't continue this journey without your light to guide me. If I could just see a glimmer of light through this infinite darkness, I'd believe you really do have a plan and purpose for me."

As I wept and released my grief to God, I noticed something out of the corner of my eye. Blinking ever so steadily, within the reach of my hand, was a firefly—one lone firefly that flickered and fluttered its way to my shoulder, where it paused and then landed. I didn't move. Then suddenly, it darted in front of me, hovering intermittently, then swooping away and then back again, as if performing a perfectly choreographed dance of light. Luminous, dazzling, glowing light!

I beheld a precious gift before me—God's tiny messenger of light—sent to pierce the darkness with a message of hope.

⸺⸺

Father, thank you for constantly reminding me that there is no
darkness so bleak that your light and love cannot penetrate.
Your night-light is always on, assuring me that
you will light my pathways with hope.

Susan Duke is a wife, mother, popular motivational speaker, and
best selling author/coauthor of fourteen books, including *Earth Angels*
and *Wolfie's Dream* (from the Schnauzer Chronicles Series).

911.....Focus!

Eva Marie Everson

*Pray for each other . . . the prayer of a
righteous man is powerful and effective.*

James 5:16 NIV

I really needed a good night's sleep.

One night I collapsed into bed, awaking several hours later.
I opened one eye, peered at the digital clock, read 4:31, and
groaned, *"Lord, why do I have to wake up so early?"*

I closed my eyes, but as usual my mind began to race—
thinking about one project and then another. Out of the blue,
the name of a national magazine publisher came to me, a
woman I barely knew.

Get up! the Lord interrupted. *You need to pray for Kathleen.*

Though tired, I didn't hesitate. God knew something I
didn't; needed something my prayers could speak into motion. I
made my way into the living room and sat on the sofa. *Father, I
don't know why you are calling me to pray for Kathleen, but, Lord,
I lift her up to you now.*

Pray for focus.

Focus? Focus at work? Focus at home? I wasn't sure. *Give her focus and direction, Lord,* I offered.

Shortly thereafter, my thoughts returned to Kathleen again. This time, I felt no call to pray, but to contact her with a letter. The following day I received a phone call from Kathleen. "Eva Marie, I just got around to reading your note. I can't believe what you wrote here! I'm almost too astonished to speak!"

That's when Kathleen filled me in on the rest of the story. While I was praying, a would-be attacker was following her as she drove to her early morning job at a radio station. She dialed 911 on her cell phone, but couldn't bring herself to press "send." Rather, she kept hearing the Lord telling her to *focus.* She did, and was able to escape, arriving safely at work.

Today Kathleen and I are good friends—and prayer partners.

───✸───

Father, create within us a willing spirit to move when you nudge us to pray. May we count it as a joy and privilege. Amen.

Eva Marie Everson's work includes *Shadow of Dreams, Summon the Shadows, and Shadows of Light.* She is a nationally recognized speaker and Bible teacher and the AWSA 2002 Member of the Year.

Show Me
Your Way

*Show me Your ways, O LORD; teach me Your paths. Lead me in
Your truth and teach me, for You are the God of my salvation.*

Psalm 25: 4-5 NKJV

$\mathcal{I}$ knelt in church on Easter Sunday 1975, sobbing. I had
promised to fly to Vietnam the next day to escort six babies
back to adoptive homes in the United States. When I'd volun-
teered to go weeks before, the war was far from Saigon, my destination. Now it raged outside the city limits. Overcome with
fear, I slumped back into the pew, put my face in my lap, and
begged God for a sign that I did not have to go. Recalling the
Easter-service scripture readings, I pleaded, "Please let this cup
pass me by."

Slowly, unexpectedly, warmth enveloped me, and my tears
began to subside. My breathing slowed to a calm pace. My

shoulders and chest relaxed as an unexplainable feeling of well-being and courage filled me. I then knew I was going to be okay. I was meant to go to Vietnam. God would take care of me. "Thank you," was all I could manage to speak, and then I left the church with my spirits soaring.

The next day I kissed my two daughters and husband goodbye, boarded a 747, and headed for Saigon filled with complete faith and confidence in my God. When I arrived I was greeted with, "Have you heard the news? President Ford has okayed Operation Babylift! You won't be taking out six babies, but 300!"

Three days later, in the midst of that chaos, the son God assigned to us—the one we had expected to adopt years from then—crawled into my arms, my heart, and our family.

—∞∞∞—

Dear God, help me to kneel before You, not only in times of stress,
but daily, asking for Your guidance. Give me the courage
to listen and then to follow Your way, trusting that Your
plans for me are greater than any I can imagine for myself.

By sharing her dramatic experiences from the Vietnam Orphan Airlift, author and speaker LeAnn Thieman motivates audiences to balance their lives, truly live their priorities, and make a difference in God's wonderful world.

The Living Word

Carol Kent

"God means what He says. What He says goes. His powerful
Word is sharp as a surgeon's scalpel, cutting through everything,
whether doubt or defense, laying us open to listen and obey."
Hebrews 4:12 THE MESSAGE

I had been busy—too busy. I had a full slate of classes and to
help with my expenses, I had accepted the position of
Residence Assistant. I hadn't anticipated the heavy load of
counseling that would accompany this position.

Monday morning, I walked into the chapel service, and our
guest speaker was Dr. Charles Woodbridge. He had white hair,
stately posture, and a commanding knowledge of God's Word.
He held the Bible as if it were his most precious possession. I
liked this man.

Halfway through the message, he said with intensity, "Young
people, if you want to know the Word of God, pick one book of
the Bible—any book—and read it every day for a month. Your
life will never be the same again!"

The Holy Spirit used the speaker's words to give me a forceful nudge. I heard God's voice challenging me to read His book. I started in Philippians. The theme of the book was *joy* and, as a student with very limited funds and too few hours in her day, *I needed joy.* The second reason for selecting Philippians was because *it was short*—I could read all four chapters in only fifteen minutes.

The first week of my reading was completed because I had made the commitment. The second week I realized that what began as an obligation became a pleasure. Paul, the author of the book, began to feel like a personal friend. By week three, I was surprised to learn that without even trying, I had memorized extensive passages from this remarkable book. When the fourth week arrived, I realized God was speaking through me to other students, feeding me the right verse at the right time.

God had personally invited me to read His Word, and He invited me to join Him in ministering His truth to others.

Heavenly Father, thank You for the power in Your Word.
I have found answers to life's questions, encouragement
for today, and strength for tomorrow as I continue
to read Your inspired Word on a daily basis.

Carol Kent is an international speaker and the best-selling author of *Becoming a Woman of Influence* (NavPress). She is president of Speak Up Speaker Services and the founder of Speak Up with Confidence seminars.

My Mazda Moment

Ellen   Edwards   Kennedy

*Fear thou not; for I am with thee: be not dismayed; for I am
thy God: I will strengthen thee; yea, I will help thee; yea,
I will uphold thee with the right hand of my righteousness.*

Isaiah 41:10 KJV

I sent up a frantic prayer as our daughter Laurie packed up
her little red Mazda, about to make the long trip to college.
That car was so tiny, and Laurie was so young. A mother's
panic seized my heart. I tried not to think about eighteen-
wheelers as I prayed inwardly, "She's my baby, Lord, about to
travel alone. There's no telling what could happen to an eighteen-year-old girl, all by herself. Please protect her!"

I knew I shouldn't be fearful—that I should put her in my
Lord's hands and trust Him. But I'd spent nearly two decades
fretting over my little girl and found it difficult to break an old
habit. The Lord understood and patiently sent a message of
reassurance to me alone.

As Laurie slammed the trunk closed and walked toward us for good-bye hugs, my eyes fixed on the letters on the back of the car. It was a Mazda Protégé. I knew the word protégé meant "one whose career is furthered by a person of prominence." But as I felt led to glance at the word a second time, there was something else I had never noticed before. The smattering of French I learned as a child on the Canadian border revealed that *protégé* also meant "protected." This was God's message to me. My worry dissolved into tears—tears of gratitude as I hugged my daughter.

Laurie noticed. "Please don't worry, Mom," she said. "I'll be okay."

"I know you will, sweetie," I said. "At least, I do now."

As she drove away, I kept my eyes on the little silver letters on the back of the car as long as I could see them and felt God smile on me.

Heavenly Father and Dearest Friend, thank You for Your infinite patience when I stumble in my faith. Thank You for the myriad gentle ways You reassure me of Your unfailing love and protection. Amen.

Ellen Edwards Kennedy is the author of the inspirational novella,
The Applesauce War, (*Harvest Home*/Barbour) and the mystery
novel, *Irregardless of Murder* (St Kitts Press).

Even the Stones Cry Out

Karen O'Connor

⎯⎯∞⎯⎯

"I tell you," he replied, "if they keep quiet, the stones will cry out."

Luke 19:40 NIV

*H*iking to the top of the famous Half Dome in Yosemite National Park was a dream of mine for many years. When I received an invitation to join a group making the ascent in August 1988, I said yes immediately. I wanted to experience it fully—to create a memory I would not forget. I spent months getting in shape with weekly workouts and learned all I could about tents, boots, backpacks, and dehydrated food.

Then the day I had been waiting for came. Halfway up the steep rock face, I took a deep breath and looked out—in front of me and to the sides, up, and down. I wanted to capture this moment forever. Everywhere I looked my gaze met a visual feast of massive pines hovering over giant cliffs, powerful boulders poised among lush greenery, and high peaks positioned against a deep blue sky. I could scarcely take it in. I realized, *This is a holy place. God is here.* I could sense Him in the grandeur I beheld.

That evening as we gathered around a campfire to rest and reflect on the day, God opened my eyes to realize that everything I needed and wanted rested there in His creation. Cool water from a rushing stream quenched my thirst. Fire under my miniature stove heated my food and warmed my feet. A cluster of boulders, some rocks, and a few sturdy tree limbs served as all the furniture I required. A bed of pine needles made a comfortable carpet for my tent. A broad old tree provided stumps for seats, limbs for hanging wet socks, and branches for shade. God was with me—in that wild place—providing, playing host to me, and sharing with me in a way I had never known before. How could I not notice His presence? Even the stones around the campsite cried out to me affirming His presence!

<hr />

Dear God, thank You for the gift of nature—trees and flowers, rocks and waterfalls. May I forever acknowledge You as Lord of all.

Karen O'Connor is an award-winning author and retreat speaker who lives in San Diego, California.

The Closet

Thelma Wells

The LORD is my light and my salvation—whom shall I fear?
The LORD is the stronghold of my life—of whom shall I be afraid?

Psalm 27:1 NIV

Waiting on the Lord does not mean doing nothing while you wait for Him to come down and rescue you. It means doing what you know is necessary to get out of the situation while confidently anticipating His help as you do it. I learned this while locked in my grandmother's closet.

My mother could never do anything to please my grandmother, whom we called Mother Dot. When I was born, my mother and I were forced out of Mother Dot's house, but my great-grandmother took me in to raise when I was two years old. As I grew older, Granny let me visit Mother Dot and Daddy Lawrence. When Daddy Lawrence was around, Mother Dot was fairly nice to me. But as soon as he left for work,

Mother Dot would lock me in the closet, just as she had my mother years before when she was a little girl.

Smell this closet with me. It reeked of tar and sweat, body odor, mildew, and mothballs. Being locked inside made me sick to my stomach.

But God is good! During those hours I felt His gentle presence as I sang songs like "What a Friend We Have in Jesus" and "Jesus Loves Me! This I Know!" There, in the dark closet, I felt God's comfort. As I sang, I felt His peace. I was not afraid. I even sang myself to sleep sometimes.

By God's grace, today I have no trauma. I have no malice against Mother Dot, for God was with me during the abuse. God is faithful. He cares about His children. Even when we're in the "stinky closets of life," we can trust Him to put a song in our hearts.

Oh, Lord. You are my Light and my Salvation.
With You, I have no fear. I praise You because
You are faithful and Your presence is real. Amen.

Thelma Wells has spoken for over twenty years and currently speaks
to over 400,000 people annually at the Women of Faith gatherings.
She is also an author, professor, and mentor.
© 1998 by Thelma Wells, condensed and adapted from *God Will Make A Way*,
"The Closet", Thomas Nelson/W, pp. 137-141.

From the Space Center

Donna Partow

He reached down from on high and took hold of me;
he drew me out of deep waters.

Psalm 18:16 NIV

*I*t was late in the day, Easter Sunday, 2000. I looked around the kitchen, strewn with the remnants of our Easter celebration: turkey leftovers, purple and pink crepe paper, little plastic cups filled with various colored Easter-egg dyes. *What a disaster,* I thought, as I collapsed on the floor. *This kitchen. My life. It's all a great big mess.*

Pick yourself up, I heard a gentle but firm voice speak to my heart.

"But I can't," I protested.

I'll help you, He said.

I reached for the counter and slowly pulled myself up. There in front of me an unopened package that had arrived a few days earlier rested on the counter. I had no idea what was inside, but I felt led to open it. It contained a cassette tape and a small note with this scribbled message: "A friend of mine asked me to send this to you. Love, Rosemary."

Rosemary didn't indicate *why* her friend had asked her to send me the tape—no clue *what* the tape was about—only the words, "Recorded at NASA, Houston, TX., December, 1999." Intrigued, I threw it into the tape recorder and pressed *play*.

The tape featured the personal testimony of Leola Glass. As her story unfolded, it became obvious that our lives had many parallels. She had lived through an experience almost identical to what I was facing at that very moment! Yet she had come through to the other side, healthy and whole. More importantly, the tape was filled with specific answers to many of the questions I had asked in recent days.

As I listened to her words, my heart flooded with new hope and confidence. I knew then, deep within, that God would also see me through my struggle. If He would go to the Space Center to bring me answers, He would go to any length to reach me.

———

Dear Father, thank You for knowing exactly what I need and when I need it. I believe that, even now, answers are on the way— some of them from the most unexpected places. Amen.

Donna Partow is the author of 14 books, including the international bestseller, *Becoming a Vessel God Can Use*. She has been featured on hundreds of radio and TV shows.

Making a Choice to Love

Kathy Collard Miller

[Love] bears all things, believes all things,
hopes all things, endures all things.

1 Corinthians 13:7 NKJV

I sensed God saying in my heart, *Tell Larry you love him.* I was shocked!

I don't love Larry and if he hears those three little words, 'I love you,' that I haven't said or thought for over two years, he might think I am approving his negligence of me and the kids. Since I didn't love Larry all the time, I believed I couldn't say I loved him at all.

As far as I was concerned, we were headed for divorce court.

God gently spoke the same message a second time, and I adamantly refused again! Then a third time the Holy Spirit whispered the message with a different twist: *Think it the next time you see Larry.*

I thought, *That's strange! But if he doesn't hear me, then he can't use it against me. All right, Lord, I'll do it, even if it's not true.*

That evening, Larry returned home, and as he walked toward me, I stared at him, gulped, and thought, *I love you*— and then after a pause, *but I don't really.*

Even though I obeyed God begrudgingly, the most amazing thing happened. Over the following months as I continued to make that loving choice, more loving feelings took over. I also recognized that I'd been holding Larry completely responsible for my happiness. My wrong thinking was changed to realize that Larry couldn't meet all my needs—only God could. In time, Larry noticed that I wasn't as angry and demanding of him and he agreed to go on a couple's retreat with me, which God used as a turning point in our marriage. That was many years ago, and we recently celebrated our thirty-third wedding anniversary. God had done the miracle of restoring our love and joy.

Heavenly Father, help me to make a decision to love even when someone doesn't seem deserving of love. That's how You loved me, so help me to pass it along.

Kathy Collard Miller is a national and international speaker whose 47 books include *Princess to Princess* and *Why Do I Put So Much Pressure on Myself and Others?*

Hugged by God

Jeanne Zornes

*He will command his angels concerning
you to guard you in all your ways.*

Psalm 91:11 NIV

*T*ense silence filled our compact car as my husband drove it
slowly through furious snow and sleet on a lonely mountain
highway. "Lord, help us get through this safely," I prayed aloud,
squinting through the front windshield. With our teens, ages
thirteen and fifteen, in the back, and home three hundred
miles away, we were hoping to find a motel in the next town.

Then I saw the headlights coming toward us, and seconds
later, we were sitting in a wrecked car with icy rain pouring
through its broken windows. "Mom!" my daughter screamed
from the back seat, seeing her brother's face, bloodied from
flying glass. The other driver emerged unhurt from his sports
van. We would learn later that he had been drinking.

Within minutes a couple in an old station wagon stopped
and offered to take the children and me to the nearest hospital,
about forty-five minutes away. My husband, also injured, would
wait for another ride.

"This has to be a bad dream," my daughter cried as we scrunched into the backseat of the couple's car. Trembling myself, I gripped her hand and reached across to my injured son, trying to keep him conscious.

"God's with us, kids," I said—for me as much as them.

"Are you Christians?" the woman asked.

"Yes," I replied.

"So am I," she said. "God sent us. We were driving to a party that we really didn't want to attend."

God sent us—with those words, my fears yielded to a strong sense of being tucked into invisible, comforting arms. I felt like God was pulling us into His lap, His hands wrapped around us like a parent calming a child after a bad dream. I sensed God's peace as doctors X-rayed my son's head, examined his broken teeth, and stitched the deep cuts on his face. Within the hour, my husband came in another passerby's car, his jaw swollen from a hard blow on impact. My injury from the seat belt would show up in a few days. Thankfully, our daughter escaped injury.

The physical scars of that nightmare night remain. But they remind me of something far better—the unmistakable sense of God's hug bringing assurance of His presence when I needed it most.

⸻

Heavenly Father, You know everything before it happens,
and can send other Christians to help me. Thank You
for embracing me with Your love when I need it most.

Jeanne Zornes, of Wenatchee, Washington, speaks and writes about God's encouragement and purpose for our lives. She's written seven books, including *Spiritual Spandex for the Outstretched Soul* (Kregel).

I Will Fear No Evil

Deb Haggerty

*Be strong and courageous, do not be afraid or tremble
at them, for the LORD your God is the one who
goes with you. He will not fail you or forsake you.*

Deuteronomy 31:6 NASB

Wincing with each tiny movement, I eased slowly from side to side trying to find a comfortable position. Hours dragged past as sleep eluded me. Earlier that day I'd been released from the hospital after an arduous surgery that kept me in intensive care and on medication far longer than anticipated. The medication and my inability to take in more than fruit juices and Italian ices made me terribly weary—if I could only sleep!

Finally I drifted off into an uneasy sleep. Seemingly seconds later, I awoke, startled! Ants or bugs crawled all over me, trying to get out from under my skin! Writhing all over, I cried. I realized I was coming down from the medicine and sugar "high" I'd been on for days.

A voice seemed to jeer at me: "See what your faith and your God have done now—all that courage and comfort He supposedly is to you—and now He's deserted you just when you need Him most! What a testimony you are!"

"Go away, Satan! God is here—I know He's still here!"

"Oh, sure He is! And what about sleep and all those crawlies? If He was here, He'd take care of those problems."

Praise songs rang through my mind; the trumpets of battle songs pierced the fog in my brain. Over and over I repeated the songs and the twenty-third Psalm, "I shall not want . . . though I walk through the valley of the shadow of death, I shall fear no evil." A warmth and peace flooded me—I knew without question that God was with me, right then! The "itchy-crawlies" eased. The notes and words of the songs chorused a battle lullaby. Finally, I slept. When morning came, I was rested and refreshed.

Thank You, Lord, for promising that You will never leave me or forsake me. Thank You for letting me sleep on Your shoulder. You are here with all of us always.

Deb Haggerty is an author, speaker, and three-year breast cancer victor dedicated to encouraging others. She lives in Orlando, Florida, with her husband, Roy, and Cocoa the Dog.

More Than Music

Fran Caffey Sandin

He rescued us from the domain of darkness, and
transferred us to the kingdom of His beloved Son,
in whom we have redemption, the forgiveness of sins.

Colossians 1:13-14 NASB

The church sat cold and lifeless as I pressed open the heavy door, reached to the sidewall, flipped the switch, and dispelled the darkness. Entering the large worship center alone on a weekday, I skipped toward the three-manual pipe organ to prepare music for the Sunday service, but that practice session became anything but routine.

First, the majestic hymn "Holy, Holy, Holy," pricked my heart. Why couldn't I just play it through and move on? The words began to sink in. Just to think of Lord God Almighty convicted me of my sinfulness in a general way, But then I remembered a time in the past when I failed to speak up in an attempt to defuse a troubled relationship. I sinned through silence, failing to obey His prompting. Grief rolled through my soul as I scooted off the organ bench and fell to my knees on the carpeted steps beside it. I sobbed, and prayed, "Dear Father, You alone are Holy, and I bow in Your Presence. I pray that you would forgive me because I have quenched Your Spirit. Lord, 1 John 1:9 says that if we confess our sins, You are faithful and just to forgive our sins and to cleanse us from all unrighteousness. I am so sorry. I want to be pure and wholly committed to You. Please—please forgive me."

As I knelt under the glow of stained glass, I could almost feel the breath of God on my cheeks and His arms around me as He whispered, "I forgive you. I love you." The nearness of His Presence lingered.

On Sunday morning, a dear brother observed, "There was something different about 'Holy, Holy, Holy' today."

I knew why. He is merciful as well as mighty.

—∞—

Dear Father, thank You that Jesus died on the cross
to pay the penalty for my sins. Give me faith to
receive Your mercy and press on with my life.

Fran Caffey Sandin is author of *Touching the Clouds: Encouraging Stories to Make Your Faith Soar* (NavPress, 2003) and co-authored the best-selling book, *Courage for the Chicken-Hearted* (Honor Books, 1998).

A Lasting Joy

T. Suzanne Eller

*Our present troubles are quite small and won't last very long.
Yet they produce for us an immeasurably great glory that will last
forever! So we don't look at the troubles we can see right now; rather,
we look forward to what we have not yet seen. For the troubles
we see will soon be over, but the joys to come will last forever.*

2 Corinthians 4:17-18 NLT

My week started with a routine trip to the doctor; an exam
that launched a whirlwind of events. Within forty-eight hours I
discovered that I had cancer and that it had spread to my
lymph nodes. Now the doctor stood at my bedside. "We found
a spot on your brain," he reported.

Then he cleared his throat and shared more bad news. "If
the spot on your brain proves malignant, you have only a
10 percent chance of surviving five years after aggressive
surgery and treatment."

That night I lay desolate in the stark hospital room. My
husband picked up the Bible and opened it to my favorite

passage. As he read, the words of Paul sank into my spirit. I closed my eyes, and soon my focus shifted from my present troubles to my ever-present God. I began to sing softly to the One who had changed my life when I was a hurting teen. I sang to my heavenly Father who had loved me when my biological father could not. I sang to my Best Friend.

The next evening the doctor ran into my room. "It's clear!" he said. The looming shadow that had appeared on the CAT scan only the day before was gone. With this good news, my statistics changed. I now had a 40 percent chance of surviving five years.

That was more than ten years ago. I celebrated my decade of survival on a rugged missions trip on the Amazon, in the Brazilian rain forest. I'm thankful for my second chance at life, yet I also realize that as a believer I win either way. Every day I live is a gift, but one day I will taste even more fully the joy I felt the night an amazing Savior wrapped me in His presence.

───

Father, Thank You for Your presence. Thank You for
every moment that I have been given, but thank
You also for the complete joy that is to come.

Suzanne is an author, freelance writer, and ministry speaker to teens, women and parents of teens. She is the author of *Real Teens, Real Stories, Real Life.*

Hospital Blessing

Linda Evans Shepherd

*Praise be to the God and Father of our Lord Jesus Christ, the
Father of compassion and the God of all comfort, who comforts
us in all our troubles, so that we can comfort those in any
trouble with the comfort we ourselves have received from God.*

2 Corinthians 1:3-5 NIV

My disabled daughter Laura, then nine years old, fought for
her life in the Intensive Care Unit of Children's Hospital as
infection seized her body.

At first I was unaware of the other critically ill children surrounding us. But as Laura recovered, one little girl caught my
eye. I watched as her broken-hearted mother hovered over this
child, the same way I had hovered over Laura.

That afternoon, as I was talking to the unit's only nurse, the
secretary approached. She said, "There is a mother in the
hallway crying; what can we do?"

The nurse sadly shook her head. "I can't leave my patients."

Perhaps the nurse had to stay, but I didn't. I went into the
hall and found the mother sprawled across the floor weeping,
the same mother I had seen in the unit.

I knelt beside her. "Can I pray with you?"

She looked surprised. "Would you?"

I bowed my head, "Lord, please help this mother. Give her strength, hope, and courage."

Then I stopped. "Can you tell me what's wrong with your little girl?"

The mother hiccupped the words, "She's—just so—handicapped."

I bowed my head again. "Dear Lord, please help this little handicapped girl be the blessing that my little handicapped girl has been to me."

I opened my eyes and saw the mother smile and wipe away her tears. "Thank you," she said.

But I should have thanked her. For as I knelt on the hallway floor, I encountered God's presence. As I prayed for this mother's child, I could see clearly that though my journey with my own handicapped child had been a difficult one, God was with me, comforting me even through the comfort, His comfort that I shared with another.

Lord, you are the Great comforter who comforts us as we comfort others. Thank you for providing opportunities to feel your loving touch. For as I give away the comfort you have given me, your comfort multiplies in me.

Linda is the president of Right to the Heart Ministry, the founder of AWSA, and the host of the nationally syndicated radio program, *Right to the Heart.*

Seeing the Light

By Ellen, as told to
Rebekah Montgomery

O keep my soul, and deliver me: let me not
be ashamed; for I put my trust in thee.

Psalm 25:20 KJV

*M*ike and I had been married only a few weeks when I discovered his problem with pornography. Not content to indulge alone, he insisted I view it too. Appalled, I sought the only safe place I knew—the Lord Jesus. With His help, I resolved to stand against my husband's evil obsession.

Angered by my determination, Mike hounded me to go to a pornographic movie with him. "Just go to one skin flick with me," he begged until I thought I'd scream.

Finally, I agreed. "Okay. Just once. But you must promise to never ask me again."

To my surprise, Mike agreed.

That night, we traveled to an X-rated drive-in theater. All the way, I prayed: "Lord, I want to be obedient to my husband, but this is wrong; and I'm trusting You to deliver me."

Mike was ebullient. As we joined a line of cars waiting for admission, I continued to pray. I felt the presence of God and heard Him say, "Watch!"

Suddenly, out of an otherwise clear sky, a bolt of lightning hit a transformer about 500-feet away. Sparks flew! The drive-in went black along with an entire section of town.

Amazed and angry, Mike turned to me. "You were praying, weren't you!"

Way to go, God! I thought.

The entire situation startled Mike. He was afraid to ask me to go again for fear lightning might strike closer! The unusual occurrence also sparked a change in him. He was eventually able to throw off his obsession, rededicating his life to the Lord. He made public confession and submitted to Christian accountability. You might even say Mike saw the Light when the lights went out!

Dear Father, You have promised to protect us from all evil. I thank You that You are my shield.

Rebekah Montgomery has more than thirty years experience as a pastor/teacher. A speaker and author of six books, she is also the editor of *Right to the Heart of Women* e-zine.
Note: The names have been changed.

Powerful Father

Brenda Nixon

—≈≈≈—

He replied, "You of little faith, why are you so afraid?" Then he got
up and rebuked the winds and the waves, and it was completely
calm. The men were amazed and asked, "What kind of
man is this? Even the winds and the waves obey him!"

Matthew 8:26-27 NIV

I sat alone by the lake; which seemed lifeless except for the barely visible ripples caused by the occasional light breeze. I stared at my reflection mirrored off the calm water. Oh God, help me! my heart cried.

A firestorm had occurred the previous day at work. I'd been wrongly accused. Another person was fired. Incensed and ready to quit, others had spoken words that could not be taken back. What had gone wrong with this—until now—enjoyable, fulfilling position? It had been my "dream" job. I had felt productive and that God was using me. Now this.

Confusion and righteous indignation battled within me. *I'll quit too,* I contended. But, my heart sank with a question: *What will I do instead?*

In this quiet refuge I brooded and prayed. Reason reminded me that God is always in control, but questioned why He'd allowed this to happen. "How can injustice be a part of your plan?" I asked the Almighty.

For years I had walked with the Lord. Always He proved Himself to be a compassionate and loving heavenly Father. This time I needed a sense of His power to protect me. After all, even my earthly father would stick up for me in the face of evil. My daddy wouldn't allow someone to hurt me.

"Well, if you're in control, God, prove it," I arrogantly challenged my heavenly Father. And prove it, He did! Instantly a loud, forceful wind filled the air. The lake responded with choppy waves that pushed the water to its shore. Trees shuddered and leaves tumbled from their branches. Then silence returned. Humility mingled with peace as I experienced my Father's strength. An immediate change came about deep within me. I was at peace.

A few months later, I was transferred to another department where I worked with a closer circle of coworkers, but not before reconciliation between my old coworkers and myself had taken place.

From that encounter on the lake, I have known He will carry me through any situation.

⸺ ∞ ⸺

Father in heaven, hallowed be Your name, Your Kingdom come and Your will be done in my heart and life today.

Brenda Nixon's mission is to build stronger families through parent education and affirmation. She is a writer, speaker, the author of *Parenting Power in the Early Years,* a wife and mother of two.

Possibilities

Dayle Allen Shockley

All things are possible to him that believeth.

Mark 9:23 KJV

One evening I listened as a minister talked about God's ability to do anything. I knew he was right, but for the past few months, I had been struggling with issues that seemed larger than life. I had made some poor choices and was now dealing with the aftermath. *Can God do anything with this mess?* I wondered.

"God wants to take your negatives and turn them into positives," the pastor said. "Remember," he continued, "A car's battery has a negative and a positive connection. You hold the negative; God holds the positive. Put them together, and anything is possible." That evening I crawled into bed thinking about those words, but was still unable to shake my remorse. I still felt like a total flop. I pulled the covers close and breathed a solitary prayer: *Lord, please make something good out of this mess I've made.*

The next morning, in an effort to cheer myself, I drove to a local antique mall. As I strolled through the aisles, a large, stunning mural painted on the back wall caught my eye. For a while I stood admiring the white stone fence surrounding a glorious array of flowers—zinnias, peonies, snapdragons, marigolds—exploding above lush jade grass. In the center, under an azure sky, a narrow pebble path led to a stately gazebo.

Suddenly, the mural moved. Astonished, I realized I had been staring at the back of two garage doors, opening out to the loading dock. My heart leaped inside of me. I knew—beyond a doubt—that God had brought me to this place to be encouraged. If a garage door could become a work of art, surely the Creator of the universe could transform my mistakes into a masterpiece!

Thank You, Father, for Your ability to turn
my blunders into a thing of beauty.

Dayle Shockley is an award-winning writer whose work has appeared
in dozens of publications. She lives with her family in Texas,
where she is a writing instructor at a Houston college.
Adapted from "Possibilities," *Whispers from Heaven,* by Dayle Allen Shockley
(Nampa, IN: Pacific Press, 1994), p. 53.

God Knows Our Needs

Betty Southard

*My God shall supply all your need according
to His riches in glory by Christ Jesus.*

Philippians 4:19 KJV

I had agonized for weeks over our plans to build a new home. My husband and I had purchased a beautiful lot on a local golf course, had the plans drawn up, and were ready to start building. But, before the work got underway, we had the opportunity to visit a mission work we supported in Calcutta, India. The Lambs, a couple who founded the mission, had become dear friends, living in our home while on furlough. While visiting them in Calcutta, I was appalled by their living conditions. I wondered if we were being good stewards by building ourselves a new home while they lived in such meager circumstances.

Driving home from work one day, I prayed again about our decision. Suddenly, I felt as if the Lord were in the seat beside me. He seemed to speak by bringing Philippians 4:19 to my mind: *My God shall supply all your needs according to His riches in Christ Jesus.* He impressed on me that He knew the needs the Lamb's were experiencing, and He was meeting them. He also reminded me that He knew my needs. If I were to keep His commandment from Matthew 6:33 ("Seek first the Kingdom of God and His righteousness, and then all these things shall be added unto you"), He would delight in providing our needs.

From that moment on, I felt peace. We built the home and used it for the glory of God—small retreats, Bible studies, and youth group gatherings. We were also able to give the Lambs a wonderful home in Arizona whenever they returned to the states. We shared the Lamb's needs with our congregation, and together we arranged for much better housing for them in Calcutta. God continued to use them both in Calcutta and in Arizona where they led many to the Lord through inviting families to dinner in their home. He supplies every need.

———

Father, thank You that you do know my needs. Help me to keep You first in my heart and trust that You will supply according to Your wisdom. Amen.

Betty Southard is a speaker, teacher/trainer for CLASS Seminars, and the author of The *Grandmother Book, Come As You Are,* and The *Mentor Quest* and Minister of Caring for the *Hour of Power.*

Out of My Comfort Zone

Jackie Holland

It is more blessed to give than to receive.

Acts 20:35 KJV

God made something of my troubled life, and it all began in a dumpster. Let me explain! Several years ago, my young son came through eating a bunch of grapes. "You won't believe this Mom," he told me, "that new grocery down the block threw boxes of fruits and vegetables in the dumpster."

When I checked out the dumpster, I found it was full of good, usable produce, just like he'd said. I filled the trunk of my car, then drove down the alley of some low-income apartments behind my church. Seeing a woman standing in the doorway of an apartment, I asked if she needed food. "It's free," I said. "It's from the Lord."

The woman stood there while I opened the trunk. But when she saw what was in those boxes, she began to cry. "I just fed the kids the last of the food this morning!" she said.

The next day I went back to the dumpster, and again it was full. So I loaded up and went back to the alley behind the church. This time a man walked out the door, his face an angry mass. My heart was pounding, and I felt like driving away; but I spoke up, "I have more food if you need it."

"Why are you doing this?" he snarled.

Fear gripped me. "Because the Lord loves you, and I love you too," I answered.

Time stood still. His big eyes filled with tears. Then the woman from the day before came outside. "I told you God speaks to people," she said to him.

The Lord blessed that man and woman with the food they needed, but He also blessed me. A failed marriage had left my life in shambles. Being used to help someone else began my much-needed healing.

Now, sixteen years later, that dumpster experience has grown into a huge food ministry, touching the lives of thousands of people. And I have learned the reality of Christ's words: "It's more blessed to give than to receive."

—☙—

Heavenly Father, thank You for allowing me to be Your hand extended. I'm just an ordinary person who loves You and believes in divine appointments and opportunities to show Your love. Amen.

Jackie Holland is the president/founder of Whosoever Will Outreach Ministries. An inspirational speaker, author, minister, and singer, she was Care Ministry Outreach Pastor at Restoration Church in Euless, Texas for fifteen years.

The Power of Intercessory Prayer

Renee Coates Scheidt

The effective fervent prayer of a righteous man avails much.

James 5:16 NKJV

"This wasn't supposed to happen, Lord!" Hurt and anger spewed from my broken heart. "Thirty-two is too young to be a widow—how can I raise these babies all by myself?" I protested.

The shock of my husband's suicide slowly became reality, though every fiber of my being resisted acceptance of such a horrific act. A wilderness I never anticipated enveloped me. How I wanted to wave a magic wand and suddenly make everything right! Yet, it was not within my power. Helpless to change the terrifying truth, I instinctively knew to whom I must turn. Only God Almighty could give the sustenance required to walk through the seemingly hopeless situation before me.

Seeking to restrain my calls to God, the enemy of my soul quickly pounced on this, his opportune moment. "See what

God did for you—after all you've tried to do for Him? Who needs a friend like that? If God really loves you, then why didn't He work a little miracle for you here?"

Without explanation, the raging battle within suddenly halted as an unnatural tranquility invaded my heart. A strange serenity whispered the words of an old hymn, *Be not dismayed whatever befall. God will take care of you.*

This is crazy, I thought. *How can I experience such a soothing calmness in the midst of such chaos?* Glancing at my watch, I saw that it was 7:15 in the evening. It was also a Wednesday night. Then it hit me. "It's prayer meeting time; God's people are praying for me!"

For the first time, I knew what it means when people say, "I felt your prayers." The peace that passes all understanding dominated my heart as my fellow believers lifted my name to Him. They prayed, and I received the blessing.

—⁂—

Thank You God for showing me the power of prayer.
Remind me to pray for others and myself as a first response,
not the last resource, when facing challenging circumstances.

A powerful, practical communicator, Renee Coates Scheidt approaches real life issues with honesty and openness, bringing hope to the heart through the truth of God's Word.

His Is the Battle!

Carole Lewis

The weapons we fight with are not the weapons of the world.
On the contrary, they have divine power to demolish strongholds.

2 Corinthians 10:4 NIV

The Bible says that Satan's mission is to steal, kill, and destroy us. It also says that God is there to fight against him on our behalf. Since the tragic death of my daughter, Shari—killed by a drunk driver—I have been able to see God's presence and power at work in my family's life.

My granddaughter, Cara, received her acceptance letter to A&M University the morning after Shari's death. She decided to put her name into the pot for a roommate, because she felt that people she didn't know would be more accepting of her if she was sometimes distant or withdrawn because of her mother's death.

Cara became aware of God's power when she learned she would have a Christian roommate and two Christian suitemates!

One of the suitemates had tragically lost her mother during her senior year of high school. She understood Cara's plight. Cara could see God moving in her life and experienced the greatness of His love for her. Although Cara feared how she might react at college, God used His divine power to demolish every possible stronghold raised up against her.

As Christians, we belong to God. Yes, the weapons of this world are terrible. But it is comforting to know that we are not the ones doing the fighting. Our family especially feels awed at God's power when we realize that God had Cara's situation worked out before the foundation of the world. We belong to an awesome God!

Dear Lord, today I want to experience Your divine power in my life. Show me Your power that I may testify to the lost world around me.

Carole Lewis is the National Director of *First Place*, a Christ centered weight loss and health program. *First Place* is used in over 12,000 churches all over the world. Adapted from "God has Great Tactics," *Today is the First Day: Daily Encouragement on the Journey to Weight Loss and a Balanced Life,* by Carole Lewis (Ventura, CA: Gospel Light, 2002), March 1 entry.

Overwhelmed by Love

Nancy Stafford

Arise, my darling, my beautiful one, and come with me. See!
The winter is past; the rains are over and gone. Flowers
appear on the earth; the season of singing has come . . .
Arise, come my darling; my beautiful one, come with me.

Song of Songs 2:10-13 NIV

Standing in the grocery store, I felt overwhelmed, blue, fat, undisciplined, and intentionally going in every direction except the one I knew I should go in. Instead of going to the gym or for a run, or quieting myself before God, I stood in the check-out line with cheese, crackers, pâté, and a candy bar. Suddenly I felt His hot breath on my neck as God invaded my mind with a whisper, *Where can you hide from my love?*

It pierced my heart.

Even in my weakness and lack of resolve, even when I despised myself, He came after me. But the biggest surprise was this: He came without discipline and condemnation. He knew the times when I had imposed enough of that on myself, I guess. Instead, He met me with love and affection.

His hot pursuit was not to reproach or scold, but to bring affection and tenderness. It blew over me like a cool breeze. It was an epiphany. I was indeed running and hiding from Him. But instead of reprimand, He brought a reminder: He pursued me to love me, to take me closer into Himself, to draw me in. And like a squirming two-year-old, I scrambled to get down from His lap.

I felt like Eve when she and Adam heard God's voice calling, *Where are you?* Like them, I hid, feeling naked and ashamed. But He spoke tenderly to me, as He did to them, *Come, come back to me and let me cover you. Let Me give you what you really need.*

I left my groceries at the store and went with Him.

—⌒∞⌒—

Father, forgive me for all the times and ways I run from You.
There is nowhere I can hide from Your love and affection.
Thank You for drawing me deeply to Yourself.

Nancy Stafford is a frequent speaker and the author of *Beauty by the Book: Seeing Yourself as God Sees You.* She co-starred on *Matlock* for five years, hosts *Main Floor,* and is a recurring guest star on CBS's *Judging Amy.* "Pursued by Love," *Beauty by the Book: Seeing Yourself as God Sees You,* by Nancy Stafford (Sisters, OR: Multnomah Publishers, Inc., 2001), p. 108.

We Bow Down

Eva Marie Everson

Like the appearance of a rainbow in the clouds on a rainy day,
so was the radiance around him. This was the appearance of
the likeness of the glory of the LORD. When I saw it, I fell
facedown, and I heard the voice of one speaking.

Ezekial 1:28 NIV

I was invited to participate in a Worship Congress, a conference where we would be learning how to worship God through
the arts. I would study under one of the top Hebrew dance
instructors by day; praise, worship, and hear the teaching of
God's Word in the auditorium by night.

The Worship Congress had also invited musicians, singers,
and banner makers. On our final night, we were to collectively
lift adoration to God unlike anything we had ever experienced
individually. During early rehearsal, I saw the two banners for our
grand finale: a bridal veil, creamy white, shimmering in silver,
and a king's robe, deep purple, gleaming with gold. As these
heavy pieces of cloth representing the Bride and Bridegroom
were ushered in, we dancers were to kneel (but only on one
knee) as music swelled behind us and singers lifted their voices.

During the performance, I felt the presence of God enter the room. Standing at the base of the stage in my final position when the banners entered the room, I dropped to my right knee. But the closer they came, the further down I went. A peripheral view told me I wasn't alone. The music reached a heavenly pitch, and the singers lifted voices like angels; there were no audible words, just the sweet sound of worship.

When I felt Someone standing over me, I attempted to look up, but could not. God's presence literally kept my head down, and I knew I was experiencing the ministry of the Holy Spirit. I continued to worship from my lowly position; and when I could finally stand, I stepped away knowing I had experienced an intimate encounter with God unlike anything I'd known before. I also knew I wouldn't be content for it to occur only once but that these moments would come when I lifted Him high and then knelt at His footstool.

Heavenly Father, I thank You for the touch of Your Holy Spirit. I bow down in anticipation of the day when You call Your church to be Your Son's Bride.

Eva Marie Everson's work includes *Shadow of Dreams, Summon the Shadows,* and *Shadows of Light.*. She is a nationally recognized speaker and Bible teacher and the AWSA 2002 Member of the Year.

My Sanctuary

Charlotte Adelsperger

*Trust in the LORD with all your heart and
lean not on your own understanding.*

Proverbs 3:5 NIV

In 1966 I drove home from another discouraging doctor's
appointment. "Why can't I have a baby?" I cried out. I longed
for a place to let go and weep. When I passed a church, I felt
drawn to go in.

I slipped into a pew and absorbed the beauty of the sanctuary.
I was alone—just the Lord and me. As I focused on the cross of
Christ, I knew He would be my listener. Silently, I poured out
how much I wanted to be a mother. Gentle peace came.

But the uncertainty continued. A year later in July, my
doctor scheduled me for surgical studies in the hospital. Two
days before the appointment, a sense of God's presence swept
over me. Like a personalized message, memorized scripture
came to me: "Trust in the Lord with all your heart and lean not

on your own understanding." (Proverbs 3:5 NIV) I was filled with assurance that I *would* become a mother!

Immediately I told my husband Bob. Then I wrote down "July 22, 1967" with notes about the experience. Prayerfully, I placed the paper in my Bible.

Unfortunately, the medical reports gave little hope of conceiving. But Bob and I continued to pray. Then in September a strange thing happened—symptoms of pregnancy! Weeks later my doctor confirmed it. I was awestruck. "God is so good!" I cried.

I shall never forget May 9, 1968 when I gave birth to a healthy baby girl, Karen Sue! When Karen was four months old, I carried her into my "sanctuary" church. "Here is where I prayed to have a baby," I whispered. "You see God, in all His love, heard me. He gave us you!" I kissed her cheek, and with blurred eyes I looked at the cross. "Thank you, O Lord, thank you!"

Almighty God, thank You for all kinds of "sanctuaries" in our lives. Thank You for Your closeness, and for faithfully meeting our needs. We praise You for who You are!

Charlotte Adelsperger and her daughter Karen Hayse co-authored
Through the Generations: The Unique Call of Motherhood. Charlotte, who has
written for numerous publications, especially enjoys speaking at women's events.

Lord, It's Your Turn

Linda Evans Shepherd

I call on you, O God, for you will answer me;
give ear to me and hear my prayer.

Psalm 17:6 NIV

"*L*et's pray for a miracle!" I told the teenagers.

"Yes!" thirteen-year-old Veronica agreed. "Let's pray that we will get a chance to share our faith with the drug runners in town."

I gulped; at nineteen I knew the dangers of such a prayer. But I couldn't lose face with the young people at the small West Texas church where I served as the summer youth director. Even so, I was relieved when, by summer's end, I hadn't had a confrontation with these dangerous men.

Near the final week, Rachel, another nineteen-year-old, joined me to help out with Vacation Bible School. After the final program, Rachel and I stood under the streetlight in the church's parking lot waiting for our ride home.

Suddenly, out of the night, I saw two of the drug runners walk by. I whispered to Rachel. "Stand very still, and maybe they won't notice us."

But the men called from the darkness, "Hey, Linda, you come over here!"

"Come to the light," I replied.

When they approached, Rachel and I made a terrifying discovery. These men were very angry and drunk. They backed us against a car and leaned over us. "Prove God is real!" they demanded.

"I can only prove it by telling you He's in my heart."

Miguel* leaned even closer. "That's not good enough," he shouted. "Prove God is real and prove it now!"

I silently prayed. *God, it's your turn.*

Suddenly the starry night changed. Lightening flashed, thunder boomed, and the wind roared. Rachel shouted above the din, "See? That's God telling you that He's real!"

The men ran one way—and we ran the other.

That night, four young people were awestruck by His presence, a presence I still feel whenever I pray, *God, it's Your turn.*

Dear Lord, thank You for being there whenever I call to You.
Thank You that I don't have to be in charge.
That's Your job. Lord, in my life, may it always be Your turn!

Linda Evans Shepherd, author, speaker, and radio personality, is the founder
and director of AWSA. She lives in Longmont, Colorado with her family.
*Name changed.

Heart of Hearts

Pamela Christian

*Delight yourself in the LORD and He will
give you the desires of your heart.*

Psalm 37:4 NIV

We'd dated for a year; I loved him like no other. Then as unexpectedly as we met, he broke off our relationship, which completely broke me. Sobbing for hours, I heard myself saying, "God, if you are everything people say, if you are able to help me, then I need you now more than ever. I need to be saved from my own mess of a life."

In my brokenness I felt God's presence and suddenly understood what this was all about. It was as if He said, *Pamela you only understand in part. I brought David into your life and took him out of your life to confirm to you that it is not an earthly relationship you deeply long for—you long for Me. You met Me once a long time ago. Do you remember? You were very little. You learned about Me when you attended church with your neighbors. I promised that I would never leave or forsake you. I know you remember. You gave yourself to Me then. But through the years My heart has been repeatedly rent because you've sought the love you need in many other ways—career, position, material possessions, and relationships. Yet, I have kept my promise.*

Though you have never acknowledged Me in your inmost heart—you only see Me as Savior for your eternal future, I AM the God of yesterday, today, and tomorrow. Now Pamela, I wait no longer. Today, I have removed from you that which you perceive to be what you deeply long for so that you can finally and abruptly see the truth about Whom and what you really need.

"Heavenly Father, forgive me," I prayed. "You are the One whom I've needed all these years! I give you my whole heart and my whole life."

And with God established as my first love, He later brought David back into my life, and we were married.

—◦◦◦—

Heavenly Father, I'm forever grateful that You made clear to me that I need You first and foremost in my life, for Yours is a perfect love, incomparable to any.

Pamela Christian is a speaker, author, Bible study teacher, and radio host who ministers the transforming power of God's Word. She and her family live in Yorba Linda, California.

No One Knows

Carole Lewis

Brothers, whatever is true, whatever is noble, whatever is right,
whatever is pure, whatever is lovely, whatever is admirable—
if anything is excellent or praiseworthy—think about such things.

Philippians 4:8 NIV

Shortly after my husband Johnny was diagnosed with stage-four prostate cancer, he shared with me that his worst fears would occur to him while he was driving. One day in a fit of anxiety, as he was driving along, he said to God, "If I only knew how long I have to live." Later, he told me that it was as if God put a billboard in front of him with only two words—*Nobody Does*. Since that day, he has had a different perspective on his disease.

The words God spoke to my husband are true. None of us knows if we will be here tomorrow. God is in control of that. Why not save ourselves some trouble and anxiety by letting Him control our thoughts as well?

Our daughter, Shari, told Johnny shortly after his diagnosis that she had also battled depressing thoughts about his cancer. Then God reminded her that everyone's future is uncertain. She could be gone before her daddy. This proved to be true when Shari was tragically taken to be with Jesus after being hit by a car, just before her fortieth birthday.

I am now encouraged to remember that Satan is a liar and loves to fill our minds with his deception. When feelings of hopelessness, worthlessness, or despair come into my thoughts, I chase them away with the truth—God's truth—by which I establish myself through prayer and God's Word.

Dear Father, help me to think about You and the truth of my situation today. Fill my mind with thoughts that are true, noble, right, pure, lovely, admirable, excellent, and praiseworthy.

Carole Lewis is the National Director of First Place, a Christ centered health and weight loss program. *First Place* is used in over 12,000 churches all over the world. Adapted from "Thinking on the Truth," *Today is the First Day: Daily Encouragement on the Journey to Weight Loss and a Balanced Life,* by Carole Lewis (Ventura, CA: Gospel Light, 2002), April 12 entry.

"Keep Looking to Me"

Charlotte Adelsperger

Find rest, O my soul, in God alone; my hope comes
from him. He alone is my rock and my salvation;
he is my fortress, I will not be shaken.

Psalm 62:5-6 NIV

While I tried to focus on a large wall clock in the hospital recovery room, my surgeon silently appeared at my bedside. Without preface, he gave the biopsy report: "It was cancer."

He went on. "I think you can keep your breast, but you have a long road ahead of you." Quickly he explained possible treatments. Tears stung my eyes, and I began to tremble.

"We can talk later," he said, squeezing my hand. Then he slipped out of the room. I wiped my wet cheek and closed my eyes. Words tumbled out of my soul, calling out to God. For a moment, I sensed someone was at my bedside. I felt warmth, a presence. Quickly I opened my eyes, but no one was there.

Then a scripture, memorized long ago, appeared in my mind: *Fear not, for I am with you, be not dismayed, for I am your God; I will strengthen you, I will help you, I will uphold you with my victorious right hand.* (Isaiah 41:10 RSV). God was holding me, quieting my fears.

After further surgery, I began five weeks of daily trips to the hospital for radiation therapy. Alone in the treatment room, I pictured Christ saying, "Keep looking intently to Me." Lying still for each powerful x-ray treatment, I recalled a scripture. It was like a sacrament—all from the Lord. Often His nearness soothed me, and thankfully, my healing has stood as a testimony to His faithfulness for more than sixteen years!

Lord God, You are teaching me how to trust You. Thank You for many healings. Thank You for the abundant life through Christ! Help me reach others with Your love.

Charlotte Adelsperger is an author and speaker from Overland Park, KS. She has written several books and for eighty-five publications and compilations. She has a personal ministry to cancer patients.

From Mourning to Morning

Louise Tucker Jones

∞

The peace of God, which transcends all understanding,
will guard your hearts and your minds in Christ Jesus.

Philippians 4:7 NIV

It had been several sad and lonely weeks since my three-month-old son, Travis, died suddenly with congenital heart disease. In fact, the weeks had now turned into months. I had held onto God with all my strength soon after his death, but now I wanted nothing to do with Him. I was so angry at God for taking my son that I vowed to never pray to Him again.

There was just one problem: my four-year-old son, Aaron. Every day Aaron would ask me questions like, "Mommy, can I go to Heaven and see Travis?" Or "Mommy, why can't Daddy go get Travis and bring him home?" I couldn't stand the thought of hurting Aaron with the bitterness consuming me.

Finally, one night, as I lay on my bed in the darkened room, I poured out my heart to God—my anger, bitterness, and pain. I prayed, "Lord, I have tried to change, but I can't. If you want me whole again, you will have to do it."

Suddenly, the room filled with an almost palatable peace, and I heard God speak to my heart, *Louise, Travis is with me.* Then, to my amazement, I felt the weight of my baby son placed against my breast and could almost feel his hair as it brushed against my cheek. I couldn't open my eyes. Tears streamed across my temples, soaking my hair. I lay absolutely still, allowing God to comfort me in a way I had never known before.

When I awoke the next morning, the bitterness and anger were gone. I still missed my son terribly. I still had no understanding of *why* he had been taken. But I had the most intimate encounter with God's love and presence that I have ever experienced in my entire life.

Holy Father, thank You for healing my hurting heart and giving me peace. I ask that You heal others who are experiencing such pain. In Jesus' name I pray. Amen.

Louise Tucker Jones is a Gold Medallion Award winning author and inspirational speaker. Married to Carl for thirty-eight years and mother of four, Louise resides in Edmond, Oklahoma.

A Clear Picture

Nancy Stafford

Surely he has borne our griefs and carried our sorrows . . .
He was wounded for our transgressions, he was bruised for our
iniquities; upon him was the chastisement that made us whole.

Isaiah 53: 4–5 RSV

I want to show you something, whispered the Lord during prayer.
A picture came to mind. I was in third grade. Crooked pigtails,
protruding teeth, and big Coke-bottle-thick glasses that magnified
my eyes like Don Knotts in his movie *The Incredible Mr. Limpett.*
Even so, every day I had to walk to the front of the classroom in
order to read the blackboard. Each trip, kids whooped and teased
"Sit down. Not again! Move your big fat head!"

So that was the picture: classmates taunting a shy, insecure
eight-year-old in Coke-bottle glasses. Yes, it was humiliating
and embarrassing, but certainly wasn't the worst thing that had
ever happened to me in my life. It seemed insignificant.

Lord, what are You trying to show me? I asked.

Another picture:

Jesus came into my classroom. He came down my row, took my hand, and walked with me to the front of the room to read the blackboard. The class got quiet; the laughing and jeering stopped. When I turned around, the teacher and kids were all smiling at me with approval and acceptance. I looked up at Jesus. He was smiling too. And—and wearing big, thick, Coke-bottle glasses!

I smiled through my tears at the mental picture. Only God could show me something so personal, so funny—and so profound. In that moment, He showed me how much He loves and accepts me, that I am created in His image. But even more, the image of Him wearing my glasses pierced me with a staggering revelation: Jesus was not only willing to die for me; He was willing to bear my humiliation and embarrassment.

He was willing to wear my glasses!

—⚭—

Lord, Help me to grasp the freedom and reality of what it means that you literally took my place. You understand. You heal. You bear my grief and carry my sorrows, so I don't have to.

Nancy Stafford is a frequent speaker and the author of *Beauty by the Book: Seeing Yourself as God Sees You.* She co-starred on *Matlock* for five years, hosts *Main Floor,* and is a recurring guest star on CBS's *Judging Amy.* Adapted from "A Healing Balm," *Beauty by the Book: Seeing Yourself as God Sees You,* by Nancy Stafford (Sisters, OR: Multnomah Publishers, Inc., 2001), p. 46-49.

My Father's Lap

Janet C. Maccaro, Ph.D., C.N.C.

If ye forgive men their trespasses, your heavenly Father will
also forgive you: but if ye forgive not men their trespasses,
neither will your Father forgive your trespasses.

Matthew 6:14-15 KJV

I am a child of divorce. For many years I felt like there was a
gaping hole in my heart where a father's love was supposed to
be. Like the adult children who were a part of the landmark
study concerning children of divorce (twenty-five years later), I
expected disaster and overreacted to mundane things concerning relationships. The fear of abandonment haunted me day
and night. I kept it all hidden very well until my health took a
turn for the worse. The stress of keeping it all together was just
too much for my brain and body to handle. In addition to physical illness, I began to experience panic attacks.

After being absent from my life for almost thirty years, my
father returned. Soon after, he was diagnosed with terminal

brain cancer and died nine short weeks later. The shock of his return mixed with the grief of his death was almost more than I could bear. Still, I felt truly blessed to have helped my father by physically taking care of him and praying by his bedside before he took his final breath.

I was asked to give my father's eulogy in front of more than three hundred friends and family members I had not seen in years. I asked God for the strength and just the right words to speak in spite of my father's absence in my life.

When I delivered the eulogy, I truly felt the angels of God standing on either side of me, holding me up. I forgave my father and felt God's healing grace wash over me. Since that day, my life has been totally transformed. I am no longer a "child of divorce." I am a child of God who can crawl up onto my heavenly Father's lap and rest my head upon His Word any time at all!

Heavenly Father, thank You for all of the divinely orchestrated moments in my life that give me opportunities to forgive and be healed.

Dr. Janet Maccaro is a respected lecturer, author and radio/television personality. She is the author of *The 90-Day Immune System Makeover,* and *Breaking The Grip of Dangerous Emotions* (Siloam Press).

Sunrise of Hope

Janet Holm McHenry

*Even though I walk through the valley of the shadow
of death, I will fear no evil, for you are with me;
your rod and your staff, they comfort me.*

Psalm 23:4 NIV

Why couldn't you let me say goodbye, God? Why?

Close to the one-year anniversary of my dad's death, I still wrestled with hurt. The doctors had given us the expectation that Dad would live up to four years after his diagnosis of Amyotrophic Lateral Sclerosis—also known as Lou Gehrig's Disease. A few months later, I took my gifted students to Oregon for a good dose of Shakespearean theater, although Dad had just been hospitalized after a fall.

As soon as I got home, however, my husband Craig had bad news. "He's not expected to make it through the night." Over the mountains and through valleys of tears, I drove almost three hours, only to hear my brother tell me, "He's with God! He's with God!"

A year later, I was still mad. As I walked and prayed one morning, I gave God a piece of my mind.

Then I watched a sunrise blossom over the Sierra Valley. Soft layers of cirrus clouds hovered like music staff lines above the mountain we call Elephant Head. Under each layer a yellow glow was turning gradually into a soft peach hue. I'd watched many sunrises during my morning walk, but I'd never seen one last a whole hour.

The sky's beauty simply impressed upon my heart that God is good. He was good to allow Dad to meet Him a little sooner than I would have liked, because He knew how Dad was suffering. God honored my dad's desires over my own prayer.

God met me that morning and answered my whys. And now, every time I see a sunrise, I thank Him for bringing a new day, a new chance, and a new opportunity to remember that He is good.

I praise You, Lord, for Your great goodness—even during the tough times. When the darkness seems to envelope me, I will remember that the sunrise is coming. Amen.

Janet Holm McHenry is the author of seventeen books, including *PrayerWalk, Daily PrayerWalk* and *Prayer Changes Teens: How to Parent from Your Knees.* She enjoys speaking about prayer and prayerwalking.

His Eye Upon Me

Jeanne Zornes

*I will instruct thee and teach thee in the way which
thou shalt go: I will guide thee with mine eye.*

Psalm 32:8 KJV

As I looked out the airplane window, I wrestled with the decision I faced about my future. After working five years for a
newspaper, I felt pulled toward short-term mission service.

Always one to check every side of a decision, I'd just visited
the U.S. headquarters office where I would be working. But
even after flying there and talking with staff, I feared raising
support and moving 1,200 miles. For a single woman, timid
about change, those challenges loomed like the mountains
below me.

I looked down at miniscule rectangles, black threads, and
moving specks I knew were houses, roads, and cars. Flying gave
God's perspective of earth from heaven, I'd always thought. Then
it struck me—God isn't just a spectator. He is intimately involved

in the lives of those people below. He sees into their hearts, and He loves them. More than that, God sees and loves me.

At that moment, I was more than a speck in a flying metal tube; I was God's special creation. He knew everything about my struggles over change. He also knew my future!

Several times in my Bible reading I'd come across expressions about God watching over His people. I never applied it to myself until that very moment. Gazing out at the gray and green landforms, all I could think about was God's eye upon me.

Far, far above this airplane, yet intimately within it, God's eye was there. I sensed a holy trust replacing my fears, as the all-seeing, all-knowing God seemed to say, *This is the way to go. Trust me, for I know.*

The next two years, as I worked at the mission headquarters, I grew spiritually in ways I never dreamed possible before. Hardships came, unknowns challenged, but I remembered He would continue to guide me with His eye upon me.

———∞———

Great El Roi—the God who sees—I trust You for the unknowns.
Your vision surpasses mine. You know what is best.
Lead and guide me in the way I should go.

Jeanne Zornes speaks and writes about God's encouragement and purpose for our lives. She's written seven books, including *When I Prayed for Patience.* (Kregel).

When Christ Takes Over

Lucinda Secrest McDowell

*My grace is enough; it's all you need. My strength
comes into its own in your weakness.*

2 Corinthians 12:9 THE MESSAGE

My first thought was: "What am I doing sprawled at the
bottom of these stairs?" Beside me, I noticed my purse in the
corner and my shoe lying nearby.

I didn't know exactly how I had fallen down the stairs, but as
I was bundled off into an ambulance, I knew I was in big trouble.

My mind raced with the ambulance. I thought about how
great the weekend conference where I was the keynote speaker
had been going. I remembered my excitement that morning as I
took advantage of a free afternoon and set out to explore a
quaint Amish countryside. A trip to the emergency room had
not been on my agenda. Now here I was—injured in an unfamiliar city. Tears streamed down my face as I prayed for God to
help guide me and be with me in this strange city.

God's promise, "Fear not, for I am with you." (Isaiah 43:5 NKJV) calmed me during the hours of treatment for a broken leg and the dread that engulfed me after hearing I'd be immobilized all of November and December.

"So, what's the subject of your presentation tonight?" the technician teased.

"God's presence in the midst of our suffering." I replied, the irony all too apparent.

That night I invited the ladies to gather around my wheel-chair. "Let's have a fireside chat about Christ's presence in the midst of suffering," I said.

And as I talked, my pain temporarily subsided. I felt a power go forth through my words; but more importantly, a peace came through my willingness to be Exhibit A of a surrendered soul. My natural responses of panic and worry faded, replaced by serenity and trust. And it almost felt like Jesus was holding my hand through the difficult flight home to my long convalescence.

A beautiful potholder quilt made by all the conferees arrived with this note, "Thanks for showing us the power of Christ to persevere and be used even when the going gets tough."

—∞∞—

Thank You, God, for literally bringing me to my knees
that I might more fully understand that You are both
the message and the hand of the messenger.

Lucinda Secrest McDowell, M.T.S., a graduate of Gordon-Conwell Seminary, is a national conference speaker and author of several books including *Amazed by Grace, Quilts From Heaven,* and *Women's Spiritual Passages.*

Never Forsaken

Cristine Bolley

He leads the humble in what is right,
and the humble He teaches His way.

Psalm 25:9 AMP

Painful events had left me feeling quite alone. My mother had moved to another state, our pastor resigned suddenly, and our beloved pet sheltie escaped our yard on a blustery winter night. For days, the hope of her return kept me from grieving her disappearance.

Months later, after the chaos of change had settled, I dreamed that I found my sheepdog lying helplessly beside the road. Starvation had caused her bones to protrude against her skin, and she couldn't open her jaws to receive the warm food that I had for her. I took her in my arms and promised never to let her be lost again.

I woke up sobbing and heart broken, finally grieving over her loss. The Lord whispered in my heart, *The grief you feel for your lost sheltie is a small reflection of the heartbreak I feel for My lost sheep. My sheep are starved too. Feed my sheep.*

Then the voice of the Lord spoke again, asking me, *What did you love about your pet?*

"I loved that she was devoted, obedient, and totally dependent on me," I responded.

I love My sheep who are devoted, obedient, and totally dependent on Me too, He said.

I wanted to remember the lesson of the dream and the words that the Lord spoke to me concerning it. Then I realized the acronym for these virtues spells *dot*. The next time I felt the loneliness of change and trials, I remembered to humble myself and admit my need of the Lord. Now I dot my i's and pray,

i am devoted to You, Lord
i am ready to obey whatever You tell me to do.
i am totally dependent on You.
Show me the way back to Your tender loving care.

Lord, neither trouble nor hardship nor persecution nor famine nor danger can separate me from Your love.
I am more than a conqueror because You love me.

Cristine Bolley is an author and inspirational teacher who enjoys intimate encounters with God and loves to help others find their way home to Him, too.

A Home For Christmas

Rebekah Montgomery

In my Father's house are many mansions . . .
I go to prepare a place for you.

John 14:2 KJV

*C*hristmas night, 1998.

God and I were having a heart-to-heart consultation as I drove my family through snow-shrouded Illinois prairies. Six months earlier, we sold our beloved home and moved into a rental property. It was a terrible wreck. For more reasons than I can explain, we desperately needed a home.

"Father," I explained, "I know You are building me a home in heaven, but I need one here too." Half-jokingly, I gave God my requirements, which were actually an "in my wildest dreams" list. On and on I went in minute detail, playfully describing a virtual mansion.

Finally, as I drove through a small town, I told God, "And it should have character, like that house!" I pointed to a large Victorian house, prickly with balconies and gingerbread, laughing ruefully at my own absurdity.

Spring came, and we still searched for a home. My husband picked up reams of information sheets, and I picked out several possibilities. Only one was of interest.

When my husband pulled up in front of this house, I gasped. It was beautiful and vaguely familiar. A tour verified that it was exactly, down-to-the-last-detail what we wanted. Surprise of surprises, the sellers took our first bid. Once the papers were signed, I stood in front of the house, and my eyes were suddenly opened. It was the house I had pointed out to God on that snowy Christmas Day! It was absolutely everything I had asked for!

My Father whispered, *See. I was listening. But wait until you see what I'm building up here for you!*

Father, I am so grateful that wherever You lead is home and You will take care of me there.

Rebekah Montgomery is a speaker and author of six books. She also edits *Right to the Heart of Women* e-zine and operates a Christian retreat house in Illinois.

Personally Chosen

Robi Lipscomb

Here is my servant, whom I uphold, my chosen,
in whom my soul delights; I have put my spirit
upon him; he will bring forth justice to the nations.

Isaiah 42:1 NRSV

At camp, the adults prayed over the room where the teens would meet. I found myself on my knees completely consumed by one thought: *Lord, am I doing this for you?*

As I prayed about my ministry to teens, I struggled to know if my ministry was a true call from God or just my own selfish desire to be in front of kids. Speaking seemed to be so much about me, even though the subject was always Jesus. I didn't want to be a fake.

So, I decided this would be the last camp, the last group of teens I'd ever get involved with. If God had anything to say about the decision, I asked that He speak to me in a personal way so that I would have no doubt that any ministry I was involved in would be solely for Him.

At the end of the session, the speaker asked the teens to come forward if they felt called to make a commitment to ministry. Three students I knew well and one I didn't know made their way to me. I shared what it was like to answer a call into ministry, asking each student to talk about which ministry God was calling them to. Then we took turns praying.

When we finished, one of the girls said, "Wait, we haven't prayed for your ministry." The tears came as I admitted I was unsure if I would continue. They all bowed their heads. The students I knew began to thank God for all the specific ways my ministry had played a part in their decision. They prayed that God would encourage, strengthen, and allow me to continue to minister to teens.

Only God could have orchestrated such a moment— designed to reassure me I was doing exactly what He'd called me to do. I cried as I sensed God's approval of my ministry, and then felt Him say, *Now keep it up.*

***

Thank You, God, that You have chosen me in a personal way to glorify You, that You hear my cries and answer me in such tender ways.

Robi Lipscomb has a passionate, "broken heart" for teens. She is the author of several articles and the volunteer coordinator of upper school chapel at Foundation Academy of Winter Garden, Florida.

"I See Jesus!"

Charlotte Adelsperger
with Alberta Heil

*You may have had to suffer grief in all kinds of trials. . . . You believe
in him and are filled with an inexpressible and glorious joy, for you
are receiving the goal of your faith, the salvation of your souls.*

1 Peter 1:6,8-9 NIV

My nephew Mark Heil, a vibrant Christian, fought leukemia
for seven years. Often in remission, he lived an active life with
his parents, Ron and Alberta, and his sister Diana. Mark put
his trust in Jesus and lived to please Him.

Mark's journey drew to a close during Holy Week, 1976. At
home on Maundy Thursday, he received Holy Communion,
which turned out to be his last solid food. On Good Friday his
nose began to bleed. It wouldn't stop. By nightfall, Mark's
doctor sent him to the hospital for blood platelets.

Mark's mother, Alberta, shared Mark's last moments with me:

At the hospital I could feel it: The doctors considered
this the end. I was weeping inside. Our Pastor Ken came
immediately. The doctor came and packed Mark's nose;
then gave him a long hug.

He's hugging him good-bye, I thought. I blinked away tears. Then a deep assurance welled up. God was in control of Mark's life. My fear melted away.

At about 1:00 A.M. on Saturday, our pastor joined hands with all of us including Mark and prayed. An indescribable peace and sweetness filled the room. Ron and I kept the all-night vigil with Mark. We held his hand and expressed our love.

By morning Mark's breathing had changed, but he was alert. "Something good has got to come out of this," he said.

"Yes," Ron said, patting Mark's shoulder.

Suddenly Mark gazed past us, looked straight ahead and said, "I see Jesus!"

Instantly we began to hug him. Victory was in the air. Mark's eyes shone. Tears streamed down my face. I cried, "Thank You, Lord, thank You!"

Within thirty minutes our son, wrapped in my arms, went to heaven. Easter morning was breaking forth in distant parts of the world, and with it, all Christ's promises of eternal life.

—⚭—

Loving Lord, thank You for the ways You enter into our
darkest moments. We give thanks for Your promises
that believers will live with You for all eternity.

Charlotte Adelsperger is an author and speaker. She has written several books and for eighty-five publications and compilations. Alberta Heil, her twin sister, is a Christian who is active with many personal ministries.
Portions of this narrative about Mark Heil appeared in *When Your Child Hurts—Hope for Parents of Children Undergoing Long-Term Medical Care* by Charlotte Adelsperger. (Augsburg Publishing House: 1985), pp. 107-108.
All rights now belong to the author. Copyright 1988 Charlotte Adelsperger.

Neon Sign

Janet   Holm   McHenry

The name of the city from that time on will be: THE LORD IS THERE.
Ezekiel 48:35 NIV

I often participate in an activity I like to call prayerwalking—good exercise, good communion with God. I had been prayerwalking on Main Street in my little mountain town for a couple of weeks when one day I decided to head out of town a bit.

I waved to the loggers headed out to the woods and the workers headed to the lumber mill. I felt an affinity for those hard-working guys. As I walked back toward town, I prayed for them. I also asked God to bless the dozen or so business owners that lined the downtown area. And then I noticed it—the city limits sign. It read "Loyalton, pop. 1,182." But suddenly I thought. What if it said, "Loyalton, A Place Where God Lives"? What if visitors were so amazed by the loving, godly people of our town that they began to ask, "What's different about this place?" I knew immediately that God had given me a vision for my town, and I began to pray that He would make it a place where His Spirit would live.

Later that evening, God confirmed that wonderful thought through His Word—the last verse of Ezekiel: "And the name of the city from that time on will be: THE LORD IS THERE." Jerusalem has many names, but this one now is the sweetest to me. The Lord is there. A place where God lives. Every ounce of my flesh sensed God with me that night—and earlier that morning—as He confirmed that He would live and breathe in my little town.

I continue to pray for the people in my town as I walk, knowing that someday they'll encounter Him as they walk in the place where God lives.

*I am so blessed, Lord, that You meet me in prayer and
Your Word. Every step I take is another opportunity
to share in Your vision for my community. Amen.*

Janet Holm McHenry is the author of seventeen books, including *PrayerWalk*, *Daily PrayerWalk*, and *Prayer Changes Teens: How to Parent from Your Knees*. She enjoys speaking about prayer and prayerwalking.

Desperate for Rest

P a m   F a r r e l

Find rest, O my soul, in God alone; my hope comes from him.

Psalm 62:5 NIV

I'd had weeks of back-to-back speaking engagements. On a trip to Colorado, I thought, *Wow, God, this is great! My flight got booked with some breathing space. I'll get there early, take a nap, shower, and feel refreshed. Thanks God!*

I arrived at the Denver airport only to discover that my connecting flight was cancelled. Stuck in the airport for five hours, I would have to dress in the airport restroom. My heart sank. *God, I just told you thanks for taking care of me. This sure isn't my plan! I'm exhausted. Show me what to do because I am so tired I can barely think.*

Walking the terminal and praying, I spotted an empty gate—one that had a door that opened to the outside, and fresh air was streaming in. *There!* I felt the Spirit whisper to my weary soul. I created my own lounge chair by placing my suitcase under my legs and my purse under my head. Then I began to read a book by A. W. Tozer about the character of God.

As I read, some birds hopped into the terminal and began to feed on crumbs. Again God's Spirit whispered, *Pam, remember,* "*Look at the birds of the air; they do not sow or reap or store away in barns, and yet your heavenly Father feeds them. Are you not much more valuable than they?*" *(Matthew 6:26 NIV) Pam, you are valuable to Me. I sent the birds to remind you that I will take care of you.*

I smiled, read the final page of my book, and drifted off to sweet slumber—in the airport! I awoke an hour later. "God this is a miracle!" I whispered. "I feel rested and refreshed!"

It was my presence, said the Spirit's whisper.

Lord, Help me remember it is in You that I find rest. When life seems too busy to stop, and sleep, help me always to at least stop and pray. Thanks for Your renewing presence. Amen.

Pam Farrel is Co-Director of Masterful Living and an international speaker and best-selling author of *Men are like Waffles, Women are like Spaghetti, Women of Influence,* and *Women of Confidence.*

Prince of Peace

Shirley Rose

His name shall be called Wonderful, Counsellor,
The Mighty God, The Everlasting Father, The Prince of Peace.

Isaiah 9:6 KJV

*S*evere headache, numbness, lack of balance, incoherent speech—all painful evidences of a body that wasn't functioning properly: My normally strong, confident husband was terrified. I sat in the neurologist's office, trying to reassure Jerry in spite of his frightening symptoms.

Even the doctor seemed fearful. He said Jerry had probably experienced a stroke or had a brain tumor. During the EEG, Jerry lay visibly shaken. I sat by his side, a trembling hand on his arm. I've never been so afraid.

But my fear was nothing compared to Jerry's. He explained later that as panic closed in, he prayed silently, "God I don't know if I will live or die, but You've promised that we don't have to be afraid. I can't cope with this fear."

Then Jerry began to mentally quote the Twenty-third Psalm. Suddenly, a supernatural peace, like a warm blanket, began at Jerry's head and flowed down his body—peace so strong it was almost tangible to him. At that exact moment, all my fear melted away. I experienced the same peace! I cannot explain it, but a sudden calmness, confidence, and a feeling akin to joy flooded me.

The doctor reported the test showed a severe abnormality in Jerry's brain. He admitted him immediately into the hospital for more tests.

But it was a different Jerry that arose from that table. He was composed, serene, and smiling. He said to the doctor in a sentence slurred by his brain, "It's going to be okay."

And it was! A week later, after a myriad of tests, Jerry was released with an ambiguous diagnosis and a very puzzled doctor. Our Lord is truly the Prince of Peace.

———

Lord Jesus, You told Your disciples "my peace I leave with you." You gave them this going away gift as You faced the unthinkable horror of the cross. I know that whatever I face, I too can experience Your peace. Thank You for this priceless legacy. Amen.

Shirley Rose is an author and speaker and created the Emmy-nominated television program *Aspiring Women*. She serves as Executive Producer and co-host.

God Cares about the Details

Kristy Dykes

Are not five sparrows sold for two pennies? Yet not one of them is forgotten by God. Indeed, the very hairs of your head are all numbered. Don't be afraid; you are worth more than many sparrows.

Luke 12:6-7 NIV

If God cares about the sparrows, how much more is He concerned about His children and the details of their lives? Traveling in a full-time speaking ministry with my husband for three years and on a part-time basis for nine years before that, my life has plenty of details! Booking engagements, office work, packing, unpacking, lugging materials and equipment in and out, traveling from place to place—even for an organized person like myself, it can be grueling. Thankfully, the Lord is always there to help, like He was one day a few months ago.

We'd only been home a day or two when it was time to leave again. That morning the finishing touch to my outfit was my gold necklace, a special piece. When I looked in my jewelry box, it wasn't there. Frantically, I searched everywhere— luggage, briefcases, book bags, even the nooks and crannies of the car—to no avail. Downcast, I prayed. "Lord, we travel and speak for Your glory," I cried out, looking heavenward. "I do my part and am very conscientious. Father, I need You to come on the scene and help me. Now!"

Immediately, into my head popped the words, *Look in the side pocket of your navy blue purse*. Wasn't that the purse I had used two trips ago? When I looked in that spot, the necklace was there! "Thank You, Lord," I gushed, my heart filled with praise. I knew those words of direction had come from Him, because I didn't remember putting the necklace there. That morning, it was as if the Lord was saying to me, *I love you, and I care about you*. As I fastened the clasp behind my neck, I marveled at the great God of the universe who cares about the details of our lives.

Heavenly Father, thank You that You care about me and the small things in my life. Help me to continually offer myself to You, to be used for Your kingdom and glory. In Jesus' name. Amen.

A former newspaper columnist, Kristy Dykes is an award-winning author and speaker. She's written nearly six hundred published articles and sold four works of Christian fiction.

A Rainbow Blessing

Dean Crump as told to
Fran Caffey Sandin

When my anxious thoughts multiply within me,
Your consolations delight my soul.

Psalm 94:19 NASB

*O*ur daughter, pregnant with our first grandchild, had called to say, "Skylar is in distress; I'll be having an emergency C-Section right away!"

Denise was only seven months along, and the baby had stopped growing. During a routine check-up the doctor discovered the underlying problem, giving Keith and Denise little hope their son would survive. He predicted the baby would have deformities and possible brain damage if he lived.

As my husband, Buddy, and I hurriedly began our four-hour drive to join them, our car became a sanctuary. We took turns quoting Scripture and praying in an attempt to stay focused on the only One who could help us, the One who held Skylar in His hands, the One who is sovereign over life and death.

Suddenly on that hot Texas day, dark clouds hovered overhead, lightning danced all around, and heavy rain pelted our windshield. We pulled off the highway to wait for improved visibility, and it seemed the unexpected tumultuous event showcased our inward emotions as we anxiously waited to hear the news.

Then almost as quickly as they came, the clouds rolled back, and the sun hit the mist to display a perfect rainbow, complete from horizon to horizon. Buddy and I marveled at this unique visual aide; and I felt God sitting right in the car beside me, reassuring us through the rainbow that everything would be okay. He calmed my spirit with unexplainable peace.

The cell phone rang just then with the message we wanted to hear, "Skylar is okay! He is tiny, but perfectly formed, looks good, and Denise is doing fine." With tears of joy and thanksgiving, we continued our journey.

Dear Lord, thank You for sitting beside us during
the trials of our lives, for giving us Your peace,
and for sending rainbows after the storms.

Fran Caffey Sandin is the author of *Touching the Clouds: Encouraging Stories to Make Your Faith Soar,* (NavPress, 2003) and co-authored the best-selling book, *Courage for the Chicken-Hearted* (Honor Books).

Gift of a Second Chance

Karen O'Connor

*If we confess our sins, he is faithful and just and will
forgive us our sins and purify us from all unrighteousness.*

1 John 1:9 NIV

"Why doesn't Lois do something about that thing?" I wondered
aloud as I looked at her bedraggled plant spilling over the edge
of the walkway above my condominium. One day I could no
longer resist the urge to clip, clip! I reached over the railing
with my pruning shears, snapped them shut around the ailing
limb, and sent it down the trash chute.

Later as I returned from the supermarket, I heard a woman
crying overhead. I looked up, and there stood Lois and her
neighbor, Nancy, discussing who could have done such a cruel
thing to her favorite plant. I knew I had to confess. "Lois," I
called, breathless, as I took the stairs two at a time. "I'm the
culprit. I'm so sorry. I should have asked first. But I . . ."

Lois listened, her eyes wide in disbelief. "You, Karen?" she asked. Nancy stood speechless. They were right. I had been cruel. It was hard to admit. I had never considered Lois' feelings.

She thanked me for being honest, dried her eyes, and we parted. The rest of the day was pure misery for me. I had hurt a neighbor, someone I liked. I prayed for guidance. *Dear Lord, I want to restore good will between Lois and me. Please tell me what practical step I can take to make things right again.* I kept silent for a moment, waiting for His answer. Then suddenly an idea came to me. There was no second-guessing my encounter with God. I knew just what to do. I jumped in the car and drove directly to the local nursery where I selected a beautiful flowering plant and attached a note of apology.

Within moments of leaving the gift at Lois' door, my phone rang. Lois accepted my apology and thanked me for the lovely new plant. I was stunned at how easy it had been to make amends. I simply had to give up my "right" to be right!

Then Lois, like the Lord Himself, bestowed on me the gift of a second chance.

O Lord, replace my prideful heart with one of compassion
and understanding so I may extend to others the
forgiveness and love You have extended to me.

Karen O'Connor is an award-winning author and retreat
speaker who lives in San Diego, California.

Safe in His Hand

Linda Evans Shepherd

Show the wonder of your great love, you who save by your right hand those who take refuge in you from their foes.

Psalm 17:7 NIV

My husband, son, and I had just left Temple, Texas, in a small plane headed back to Colorado. We were ten thousand feet in the air when the monotonous drone of the engine broke with silence. I turned to my husband, Paul, "What's happening?" I asked.

"I don't know," Paul said, adjusting the controls. The plane sputtered then died again.

"We can glide for a while," Paul said. "Maybe I can find a place to land."

I closed my eyes to pray. "Lord, help us."

With my eyes closed, it was as if I saw the hand of the Lord holding our plane in the air. He spoke in the quietness of my heart, *Linda, do you trust me?*

"Lord, it's a lot easier when the engine is running," I replied.

Linda, when you are in My hand, you couldn't be safer.

The engine roared back to life, sputtered, and died repeatedly until the Waco airport was in sight. Paul dropped the landing gear.

Just as the plane touched the runway, the plane died again. We rolled to a complete stop, right in the middle of the runway.

The control tower came on the radio, "Aircraft, you must exit the runway; you're in harm's way."

Paul replied, "Sorry tower, we are without power."

A few minutes later, as a truck towed our plane off the runway, one of the plane's wheels popped off. The plane tilted as the landing gear dug into the pavement.

What if that had happened when we were landing? I wondered in horror.

Once again I heard His voice: *You were never in danger, for you were in the palm of My hand. Trust Me.*

I closed my eyes and prayed, "Thank you, Lord, for it's into Your hand I commit my life. No matter the circumstances, there's no safer place to be."

—⟡—

Despite my life's circumstances, I choose to trust in You, Lord.
Despite the fiery darts of the enemy, You are my shield.
Lord, keep me in the palm of Your hand.

Author Linda Evans Shepherd has a national speaking ministry and directs the Right to the Heart of Women Conferences for women ministry leaders.

Threads of Hope

Fran   Caffey   Sandin

"But if any of you lacks wisdom, let him ask of God, who gives to all men generously and without reproach, and it will be given to him."

JAMES 1:5 NASB

"*G*et out of here! You don't know what you're doing! I hate this place!" Those were among Hattie's milder statements to hospital personnel. The elderly woman in Room 225 had undergone orthopedic surgery, and it appeared she would be hospitalized for a long time. Her gruff, ill manners and obscene language sent me, a new graduate nurse, fleeing from her bedside.

After work one day, I prayed and asked, "Lord, how should I deal with this difficult patient?"

Suddenly I felt overcome with compassion, and the Lord's presence seemed near as He opened my spiritual eyes to her real needs. After this encounter, I felt more confident and even excited as I entered Room 225 the next morning.

"Hattie, I have a question for you," I began. "What do you really enjoy doing?" After a few off-color remarks and her usual gruff attitude, I probed further. "No, I mean—do you have any skills like sewing or painting?

Hattie perked up when I mentioned sewing. "I used to crochet real good, but I haven't had the money to buy any thread in a long time," she said pensively.

"Let's make a deal, Hattie," I said. "If I buy the thread, would you crochet some doilies for me? I'm a newlywed and could use some decorations."

"Sure, honey! Just buy some thread and bring it to me." I continued to pray as I set off to shop for Hattie. Peace began to replace anger and frustration as I thought about this poor woman whose words and actions were yelling through the megaphone of life saying, "I am lonely, and feel so unloved and unappreciated."

Hattie's eyes brightened and her countenance gradually began to change as she completed her beautiful doilies. God knew her needs. I just had to ask Him.

Dear God, Please help us look beyond the words and actions of others to understand the reasons. Help us to be sensitive to ask for your wisdom in dealing with all our difficult relationships.

Fran Caffey Sandin is the author of *Touching the Clouds, Encouraging Stories to Make Your Faith Soar* (NavPress, 2003). She is a nurse, organist, writer/speaker, and grandmother living in Greenville, Texas.

The Flip Side

Gayle Roper

"People judge by outward appearance, but the LORD looks at a person's thoughts and intentions."

1 Samuel 16:7 NLT

My husband is very organized. He carefully plans and allots his time to finish any project ahead of deadline. I am not organized. Time always gets away from me, and I find myself rushing to get things done at the last moment.

Chuck is very good with money; however, money runs through my hands like sand through an hourglass.

Chuck rarely forgets. I can ask him to run an errand, and he will always remember. I am as likely to forget as not. Once when I forgot to pick up the dry cleaning, he asked with frustration, "Do you do this on purpose?"

Much as I hate to admit it, this talent comes naturally.

Chuck always turns out lights when he leaves the room, even if I'm still in it. He always locks the car, and I can't count the number of times I've gone to use my curling iron only to find Chuck has unplugged it and put it away.

You might think the above are sterling qualities in a spouse, but try living with them year after year. Once when the lights went out on me one too many times, I started fuming about how rigid he was, how regimented.

And the Holy Spirit nudged me: *You can center on the negative aspects of his traits if you want, or you can look at their flip side, their good side. That discipline of his means there's always money in the bank, gas in the car, and repairs made as needed. Look at his heart, Gayle, as I do, not his trying habits.*

God taught me to see Chuck not as someone out to make my less structured life difficult, but as a gift to make my life secure, safe, and less stressful. It made an already fine marriage that much more of a delight.

———

Lord, You have made us different so we may fill each other's holes. Give us grace to center on the good side, not the negative side, of those we love.

Gayle Roper is the author of more than thirty books and has been published in magazines including *Discipleship Journal, Moody Magazine,* and *The Christian Communicator.* She teaches at writers' conferences and speaks for women's events.

A Calm in the Crisis

Joan   Esherick

God is our refuge and strength, an ever-present help in trouble.
Psalm 46:1 NIV

*I*t was a glorious weekend in April—eighty-five degrees, cool ocean breeze, brilliant warm sun, and cloudless blue sky. My sister, our five children, and I had just arrived for a moms-and-kids-only weekend away in Hilton Head, South Carolina. Exhausted from the long drive, I was ready to snuggle in for a nap on the beach while the kids bodysurfed in the gentle, rolling waves.

As I closed my eyes for much-needed rest, something in me said *Don't sleep, Joan. Keep your eye on Dan.* I craved sleep, but my inner prompting kept nagging, *Keep watching Daniel.* So I slouched in my beach chair, kept my eyes open, and watched my seventeen-year-old firstborn.

Not ten minutes into my vigil, Dan turned, looked at me, screamed for help, and collapsed into the water fifty yards away. He was having a full-blown seizure, something he hadn't had since his seizure disorder had been brought under control years earlier.

I shot out of my chair and sprinted into the waves. My fourteen-year-old daughter, Sarah, got to Dan first and pulled his head out of the calf-deep tide. By the time I arrived, he was convulsing. I rolled Dan onto his side, cradled his head, and started timing his convulsions, something I'd long ago learned to do. As I watched and counted, I whispered, "Father, be with us."

The second I cried out to God, I felt His presence. He cradled my heart as surely as I cradled Dan's head. His cradling protected me from swirling emotions the way mine protected Daniel from swirling tides. I knew God was with us because I was overcome with a peace beyond my circumstances and myself—an unnatural calm in the crisis. In that moment, I knew God was near. Thankfully, Daniel's seizure passed, and his medications regained their effectiveness in preventing further episodes; but the sense that God is watching over us and determined to keep us safe remains.

※

*How precious is Your presence, O Lord! Help me to
remember You in crisis or calm and sense Your
cradling in all circumstances that swirl about me.*

Joan Esherick, an author, speaker, and freelance writer,
lives in southeastern Pennsylvania.
Adapted from "God's Open Arms: The Drawbridge of Faith,"
Our Mighty Fortress: Finding Refuge in God, by Joan Esherick
(Chicago, IL: Moody Publishers, Inc., 2002), pp. 23-24.

Can I Still Hear the Music?

Rebecca Barlow Jordan

At night his song is with me—a prayer to the God of my life.

Psalm 42:8 NIV

*A*s a young mother, I asked God to give me a song—a simple melody that could put a smile on my heart when all known instruments of joy were silent.

I first heard the melodies beside a Colorado river. For many summers, I sat listening as the early-morning sun peeked over the blue horizon and a chorus of aspens whistled by the water. As I poured over familiar scriptures, it was as if notes began to dance on the page by an invisible hand. An inaudible voice whispered, *Come—and the music will begin.*

A few notes, then a full-scale melody escaped my lips—so softly only the Lord and I could hear. Like the "Jesus People" of the 70s, I simply took a verse of scripture, humming a simple melody. God did the rest.

Years passed, and I wondered, *Can I still hear the music—at home?*

So not long ago I headed out to my backyard hammock and opened my Bible to Psalms. I breathed a prayer and asked God for another divine encounter. At first I heard only a fussy squirrel, a noisy blue jay, and distant car horns. But as Jesus silenced my heart, the notes were unmistakable. I looked up, awed, as heaven played its harmony with my crude efforts.

That's when I discovered the secret Jesus was trying to teach me: Music does not just whisper through the mountain forests and peaceful rivers. It will stream behind the raging rapids and burst through a splitting earthquake. Melodies are not locked inside romantic hideaways or tucked away in some forgotten corner. It does not take an orchestra to raise a heavenly symphony. It only takes one listener, for music is in the ears of the beholder—and in the heart of the Lover.

Heavenly Father, even when the notes fade, You never leave.
Still my heart often so I can hear the melody.
For You are the song. You, Lord, are the music.

Rebecca Barlow Jordan, a speaker and best-selling author, has written over 1600 inspirational works and numerous books, including *At Home in My Heart* and *Daily in Your Presence*. © 2001 by Rebecca Barlow Jordan, condensed and adapted from *At Home in My Heart: Preparing a Place for His Presence*, Promise Press, a division of Barbour Publishing, pp. 115-125.

Just Let Go

Barbara Hibschman

The eternal God is your refuge, and
underneath are the everlasting arms.

Deuteronomy 33:27 NIV

I was only twelve years old; but after some instructions, I proudly started the tractor engine. Daddy needed my help. His tractor was stuck in the mud, and he wanted me to drive the other tractor so he could connect them with a chain and pull his out.

However, when I proceeded down the hill my joy turned to fear. The needles on the gages swayed back and forth. The brakes didn't work, and I couldn't shift gears. The tractor was out of control. I went faster and faster down the hill. I looked back at Daddy and saw him running after me, waving his arms and shouting, "Don't be afraid. Let go. Jump!"

I jumped, and immediately Daddy's strong arms cradled my trembling body. He held me close as we watched the tractor hit a tree.

Years later I stood beside Daddy's hospital bed and watched needles dance back and forth on monitors. Like the old tractor, his physical body was out of control and trying to gain release from what didn't work anymore.

As I watched Daddy's body go "downhill," God brought the tractor incident to my mind. I sensed a fresh awareness of His presence. Sweet words of His promises caused me to focus on heaven, and I caught a glimpse of my Lord with outstretched arms waiting for my daddy. I felt those same loving arms embrace me when I faced the reality of letting go of his earthly life.

Confidently, I took hold of Daddy's hand, and in my heart I waved for him to jump. Then I leaned down close to his ear and whispered, "Don't be afraid, Daddy. Just let go."

Heavenly Father, thank You that You are always near,
and that Your everlasting arms are strong enough
to hold us when we need to let go. Amen.

Author and speaker Barbara Hibschman is an effective communicator with a passion "to know Christ and make Him known." Her audiences include women's ministries, Christian education, missions, and writers' conferences. Adapted from "Just Let Go," by Barbara Hibschman, taken from: *My Turn to Care—Affirmations for Caregivers of Aging Parents* (Drexel Hill, PA: Ampelos Press. 1994), pp. 216, 217.

Where'd You Go?

Victorya Michaels Rogers

Do not be anxious about anything, but in everything, by prayer
and petition, with thanksgiving, present your requests to God.
And the peace of God, which transcends all understanding,
will guard your hearts and your minds in Christ Jesus.

Philippians 4:6-7 NIV

I had looked forward to getting a new puppy. I just love their little faces, their baby teeth, and their rambunctious energy—so precious. With great anticipation I picked up six-week-old Ashley at the humane society and took her home.

A rude awakening followed. During the first week, I was amazed how something so cute could be so much work! Obviously my only desire was to love and nourish my sweet new pet. But she didn't seem to know that. She only knew she had once felt secure with her mother, and now she was alone in a strange place. As long as I was visible and at her side, she was happy and content. Every time I stepped away, even just a few feet away, she would begin to cry, terrified that she had been abandoned. Every time I put her in her crate to sleep, she would howl and whine.

By the fourth night, my nerves were completely rattled. Then it hit me. Isn't that how Jesus must see me sometimes? He's right at my side loving, nourishing, and protecting me. His presence is all I need to feel secure, but I let my fears and insecurities keep me from relaxing and resting in His care. Oh sure, there are times when it seems like God is right there saying, *I love you; I have a plan for you.* And there are times in my morning devotional when a scripture will seem to be speaking just to me.

But the minute things get scary, stressful, and unpredictable, I panic and begin to cry, just like my sweet puppy. How quickly I forget that Jesus hasn't gone anywhere. He hasn't abandoned me. He still sees me and knows exactly what I need.

Dear Jesus, help me not to be anxious. Reveal to me, right now, that I am not alone. Please give me the peace that passes all understanding in the midst of my storm. Amen.

Former Hollywood agent Victorya Michaels Rogers speaks across America and lives in Oklahoma with her husband, Will, and two children, Matthew and Katie.

Peace, Be Still

R e b e c c a   B a r l o w   J o r d a n

*The disciples went and woke him, saying, 'Master, Master,
we're going to drown!' He got up and rebuked the wind and
the raging waters; the storm subsided, and all was calm.*

Luke 8:24-25 NIV

How can you sleep? I thought, as I stared at my husband,
dozing soundly. *It's after midnight, and our daughter is not home.*

Fear began to seep in, like water in a leaky boat. At 12:30
A.M. I woke my husband. "Something's wrong," I said.

We had given our daughter and her date permission to fish
at a nearby lake, but cautioned them to leave the park before
sundown. We had no idea what could have happened.

We called the father of the young man our daughter was
dating and discovered the two had rented a boat. That had not
been part of our agreement. One more hour had passed. My
mind began to form disturbing mental images of muggings,
overturned boats, and floating bodies washing ashore. I cried
out in prayer, "God, keep them safe!" and began to pour over
Psalm ninety-one, our family's favorite comfort Psalm.

My husband met the young man's father out at the lake. About 2:00 A.M. he called to tell me they had found the car— but the children were not in it. The park police and the marina owner were called, and the search went on.

What if the boat capsized? I thought.

"I know you're here, Jesus," I cried. "But please, be there— in the boat with them too."

An hour later the phone rang. I heard the sigh of relief and joy before my husband ever uttered, "They're safe." His voice continued: "Water in the boat . . . stalled motor . . . Good Samaritan happened by . . . " What I heard in the blackness of that night was a divine whisper from the Master Himself to my storm-tossed heart: *Peace, be still.*

At 4:00 A.M., when my daughter walked into my arms, I realized God had stilled the storm within, and I knew we had encountered His divine presence once again.

Lord, time and time again, You have stilled my storms and calmed my fears. Thank You that when You are in the boat, I can have peace in my heart.

Rebecca Barlow Jordan, a speaker and best-selling author, has shared God's faithfulness in over 1600 inspirational works and numerous books, including *At Home in My Heart* and *Daily in Your Presence.*

God Is Faithful

Susan B. Wilson

"For I know the plans I have for you," declares the LORD,
"plans to prosper you and not to harm you,
plans to give you hope and a future."

Jeremiah 29:11 NIV

*N*early three years ago, during my prayer time, God convicted me to "get off of the phone."

It seemed His message to me was to do less marketing for my business and to provide more parenting for my children. Dismayed, I thought, *Okay, Lord, but what about my business?*

But God put a peace on my heart that I wasn't to worry; He would take care of my business. However, I'd observed that God's care of my business was not quite the way I'd envisioned. For my business was no longer growing; instead, it shrunk.

Memories of former challenges and great financial outcomes gave me all the ingredients I needed for occasional pity parties. After all, my self-pity was justified since I had made major self-sacrifices for my children.

I was in the midst of a pity party when I felt God speak to me once again. Though I hadn't really invited Him to stop by, He showed up. So, I thought I'd voice some of my hurts and frustrations—again.

This time, as I rehearsed my grievances, I felt the Lord jump in. (I guess He wanted to make it more of a conversation!)

He impressed three convictions on me. He reminded me that my life isn't about me anyway—my life is for His glory. Secondly, He reminded me that my children are now more joyful, confident, and more in love with Him. And finally, the Lord admonished me to quit referencing my choices as sacrifices. Specifically, I felt the Lord saying, *You have not made sacrifices. You have made more room for the joys I have added to your life*.

My joys *are* Reid and Breanne. The Lord only gives Truth. Praise God that He has the final Word.

Lord Jesus, thank You for Your Word of Truth, for Your Presence of Truth, and for Your Holy Spirit that guides us in Truth. Thank You for Your plan. Amen.

Susan Wilson's books include *Goal Setting, Accelerated Goal Achievement, Your Intelligent Heart,* and *Gourmet Meetings on a Microwave Schedule*. She also has contributed to four additional books. Susan is a nationally recognized speaker and facilitator.

I Want That Refund!

Kathy Collard Miller

[Jesus said,] "No one can serve two masters. Either he will hate
the one and love the other, or he will be devoted to the one and
despise the other. You cannot serve both God and Money."

Matthew 6:24 NIV

*L*arry and I had made a major purchase from a Christian business. Later, they informed us they couldn't supply the item and
promised a refund. When we didn't receive the refund after
repeated requests, I was furious. I couldn't believe God would
want His money treated this way—especially by people who
called themselves Christians!

One day as I had my devotions, my thoughts again turned to
the situation, and my anger returned. I wrote in my journal,
"This is a test of whether we are stewards or owners of God's
money. Father God, this is not hidden from Your sight, and
neither are Your eyes closed and uncaring. Thank you that I
can surrender this to You."

I decided to find a verse to memorize so that when my anger welled up again, I could meditate on that verse. The Lord whispered in my heart, *Look at Jeremiah 16.* At first I resisted because I knew that passage didn't deal with this situation. But when He whispered it again, I turned there. At the top of that page, a verse I'd marked in yellow many years earlier caught my eye. "My eyes are on all their ways; they are not hidden from me, nor is their sin concealed from my eyes" (Jeremiah 16:17 NIV).

Those were some of the very words I'd just written in my journal! God was telling me that He truly was aware and that He was with me in that moment. He wanted to help me have a godly response to the situation. From that time on, whenever my anger returned, I again sensed God's presence and His affirmation that He cared about us and His money!

In time, we did receive the refund, but I had encountered God and His priorities.

Father God, You are always with me, but thank You for those special times when You speak directly to my heart. You are big enough to be aware of all my struggles.

Kathy Collard Miller is a popular conference speaker and the author of forty-seven books including *Princess to Princess* and *Why Do I Put So Much Pressure on Myself and Others?*

Whispers of Hope

Sherry M. Jones

Behold, I am coming soon! My reward is with me, and
I will give to everyone according to what he has done.

Revelation 22:12 NIV

Startled by a horrifying nightmare, I opened my eyes in the intensive care unit. I felt like all the life had gone out of me as I listened to the beeping of my own heart monitor. *Why did this accident happen? Why is Ken gone? Will I survive the injuries? The cancer? Will I walk again? What do I possibly have to live for?* I cried out to God.

The reality of the situation was unbearable. A massive train collision only a few short hours earlier had ripped my newlywed husband from our handheld embrace. Now I could see no possible recourse, no way out. I squeezed my eyes tightly for the last time and pleaded for God's mercy. *Take me home, Jesus! Please take me home!*

In my deepest hour of despair, I gave up on life. Yet, my heavenly Father answered my cries in ways I never imagined. The room became silent. The loving voice of the Holy Spirit softly whispered hope in the broken crevasses of my heart, *Tell my people I'm coming soon. And, tell them to be good to each other.*

Time stood still as I, covered with a blanket of indescribable peace, savored each word and closed my eyes. Although the physical pain endured, I knew God's presence would never leave me.

Despite the loss, the grief, the pain, the cancer, and the extreme brokenness, God allowed me to see a future filled with promise. I yearned to heal. I knew He had called me to tell His people that regardless of the hopelessness of their circumstances, life is a gift and the glory of Jesus' coming awaits all those who believe and call upon His name. Showered with hope, I learned that the desire of God's heart is for us to cherish our relationships and to be good to each other.

Dear Heavenly Father, during my deepest hour of despair, You cradled me with loving-kindness. Create in me a pure heart to serve You and to minister Your glorious hope and resurrection. Amen.

Sherry M. Jones, MA, is an author, nutritionist, doctoral candidate, and national speaker, seen on *Oprah* and *The 700 Club*.

Four-Wheeled Answer to Prayer

Silvana Clark

On the mountain of the LORD it will be provided.

Genesis 22:14 NIV

*I*t all began when our ten-year-old, Sondra, was asked to be a spokeschild for Childcare International, a Christian relief agency. They sent her to Africa, where she saw first hand the horrors of people dying from AIDS. Sondra visited schools and danced with children who had lost both parents to AIDS. Our blonde, Caucasian daughter hugged children who were fascinated by the color of her skin. We were so shocked at the poverty of these children that we left all our clothes and suitcases with them. Upon returning to the comforts of home, Sondra began speaking in churches, asking people to sponsor a child for $30.00 a month. She quickly raised $35,000 for Childcare International.

Allan and I felt an obligation to do more. Over and over again, we thought about ways to let additional people hear how they could help children in Third World countries. "Let's take a year and travel around the US, speaking at churches across the country," my husband suggested.

"Do you really think we can pull this off? Are you sure God wants us to take a whole year and travel the U.S.?" My husband Allan and I talked late into the night, wondering if we were both hearing the same message from God. Why would He ask us to leave our comfortable home, jobs, and friends to live in an RV?

Of course, there was one *big* problem. We didn't have an RV to live in, and we didn't have a truck to pull our non-existent trailer. We prayed. We waited. We prayed.

One day a letter arrived from Jayco RV. "Our company would like to help you in your worthy adventure." They sold us a twenty-eight-foot, fifth wheel trailer at cost, the exact amount we could afford. After my husband assured me he was not capable of pulling the RV behind him like a plow, we continued to pray.

Then the phone rang. "Happy Birthday, Sondra! This is Jerry Chambers from Chambers Chevrolet. We heard how you plan to travel for Childcare International, and Chevy would like to help. We are giving you a brand-new, top-of-the-line truck with a diesel engine to use for your trip around the US."

Now that's heavy-duty answered prayer—and an intimate encounter with God's power!

Thank You God, for surprising me as I pray. Let me continue to know You love me and will always provide for me.

Silvana Clark is an award winning author and motivational speaker. She conducts keynotes for businesses around the U.S., Canada, and overseas, while traveling the U.S. in an RV.

Beyond My Vision

Kari West

Great is His faithfulness; his lovingkindness begins afresh each day.
Lamentations 3:23 TLB

Thick fog swallowed San Francisco's skyscrapers and my spirit as I scurried from night school toward home. Rancid smells and cigarette smoke drifted across sidewalks. Strangers peered through windows and catcalled from storefront doorways. I shivered more from fear than from the chill.

Home was a rented room on the eleventh floor of a boarding house—three thousand miles from my family. I was eighteen, working days to pay for room, board, and tuition. Pulling the shade on the room's only window, I listened to the growl of buses on Market Street and stared into the dark eyes of the night. So many people living in this big city, yet I felt so alone. How I longed to hear a caring voice!

But only the wall heater made a sound, crackling as I sorted the mail and read my mother's latest letter: "Remember that the sun goes down each evening but always comes back up in the morning—even when you can't see it," she encouraged. Drifting off to sleep that night, I tried to imagine the sunrise.

When the alarm rang, I rushed to the window. Mother was right! That morning an apricot globe peeked through the mist and banished the night. My heart leaped in the light of its rays. I stood nose to glass, transfixed not so much by its glow as by the warmth of a deep, inner knowing that the God I had believed in since childhood was with me right there in my tiny room that very moment.

Later, during my brisk walk to work that morning, I felt enveloped with an assurance that wherever I went in life and whatever happened to me, I would not go alone. God would remain who He has always been—my caring Creator and Heavenly Father, even when the night seems dark and lonely.

Like pregnant Hagar in the wilderness, I'm so glad
You are the God who sees. Teach me how to align
my sight with Yours and to faithfully live out the
purpose You are birthing in me—no matter what.

Kari West, author of *Dare to Trust, Dare to Hope Again: Living with Losses of the Heart*, lives in California with her husband, two dogs, and a goat named Sigmund.

The True Judge

Eva   Marie   Everson

Bless the LORD, O my soul; and all that is within me,
bless his holy name. Bless the LORD, O my soul, and
forget not all his benefits . . . The LORD executeth
righteousness and judgment for all that are oppressed.

Psalm 103:1-2,6 KJV

Though our daughter had custody of her happy and healthy little girl, the father's family hired private investigators. In the space of one week, we were hauled into court on two separate trumped up charges of neglect. With the "evidence" they had, it looked hopeless.

The night before the hearing, my heart never stopped praying. I don't know when I fell asleep, but I awoke at four o'clock in the morning.

Get up, God instructed. *I've something to show you.*

I rose and walked into the living room. My Bible was lying on the coffee table, so I opened it and began to read. *That's not it,* He whispered. I turned the television on to watch a segment of a popular evangelist, but still God whispered, *Not it.* Out of the corner of my eye I noticed a devotional book lying on the end table next to my chair.

Open it.

I obeyed, opening it to a reprint of Psalm 103. The words stirred up a fire within me. *I am the One True Judge*, He continued.

I knew then, nothing we'd done—good or bad—could control the outcome of that day's hearing. Only God was in control.

When I arrived at the courthouse, my daughter walked in just after me wearing joy like a warm cloak. "Everything is going to be okay," she told me. "God told me so." I shared my experience with her, and then we sat and waited for God to prove Himself faithful.

The attorneys were called into the courtroom—just the attorneys. Three minutes later, they returned; my daughter's attorney was smiling. "He's thrown it out," she said. "He doesn't even want to hear it."

When God said *Get up*, I got up. It's wonderful how many burdens He takes from us when we obey the command of His voice.

—◦◦◦—

*Thank You, O Ruler of nations and kings, that You
hold all things dear in Your hands. I praise You for
who You are. There is none above You. You are God.*

Eva Marie Everson's acclaimed series of articles, "Falling Into the Bible" (Crosswalk.com), were written after her recent trip to Israel. She is a nationally recognized speaker, Bible teacher, and the AWSA 2002 Member of the Year.

Undisciplined . . .
Who, Me?

God has not given us a spirit of fear, but of power
and of love and of a sound mind.

2 Timothy 1:7 NKJV

*M*y clothes were a little tight. I was slightly behind on a
deadline for my next book. My house was clean—underneath
the clutter. A small voice of discontentment nagged at me. I
made time for God, but some days I crammed Him in after a
full day. I felt out of balance, discontented; but I couldn't quite
put my finger on it.

One day I sat in the recliner in front of my TV munching on
kettle corn. God interrupted Judge Judy. *Undisciplined*, He said.

Who, me?

Perhaps God hadn't noticed all the activity I generated.
Couldn't He see that I was writing my second book? Had He
missed the fact that I ministered to teens?

I finally abandoned my façade and confessed that I had acquired some poor habits. As I knelt in prayer, I let God speak. I was forced to take a long and honest look at my life. At forty-three, I was an empty nester. I was used to competing with noise and energy and a full house. The mindless activities had become time-fillers. The sad thing is that they'd also become time-killers that left me restless and unfulfilled.

I decided the only way to rid myself of the bad habits was to eliminate them entirely for a period of time. I went on a twenty-one day, time-stealer fast, and asked a few friends to pray with me as I opened my day to God and let Him reorganize my life.

When the twenty-one days were over, I realized that I had pockets of time to pursue what I loved—time with God, moments in my garden, writing a chapter on a new novel.

God had more for me, not a legalistic list of tasks to perform, but a new way of thinking, seeing each moment as an opportunity to fulfill His destiny for my life.

Father, help me to look at my life with Your flashlight. You are not a taskmaster, but You are a God of purpose. Help me to avoid the time stealers that rob me of those destiny moments.

T. Suzanne Eller is a speaker and author of *Real Teens, Real Stories, Real Life.* When not writing, Suzanne can be found riding horses.

True Forgiveness

Karen Porter

———∞∞∞———

Do not repay evil with evil or insult with insult, but with blessing.
1 Peter 3:9 NIV

*F*our of us met every week clinging to one another's faith, hoping to ease our pain. A church youth leader had plunged into unspeakable sin. We watched our teenagers grapple with hurt and disappointment. And we were angry. We could never forgive him. He deserved to be punished. We hoped he was miserable.

Each week, we worked our way through the book of Jonah, watching God intervene in the reluctant prophet's life. When we came to the last chapter, we mocked poor Jonah a bit. Sitting out there on the hill. Whining. Pouting. Then someone said, "Jonah's big problem was that he didn't want to forgive those Ninevites."

I suddenly saw myself on that hillside sitting beside Jonah and heard God's quiet voice mock my indignation. *You won't forgive either, will you?*

I went to my knees and then to my face—lying flat in the presence of my Holy God. God laid his loving arms around me that afternoon and put forgiveness in my heart. He helped me pray, "Lord, please bless that person who has hurt me. Please give him a wonderful ministry and a joyful life."

Only God could have pulled me from that black hole of anger. Real forgiveness comes when you are able to release the people who hurt you and ask God not to punish but to bless them. Only a direct encounter with God could cause me to forgive like that.

I looked around. My friends were also on their faces begging God for a forgiving heart—asking aloud for God to bless the offender. We all smiled through our tears, and someone said, "I feel free." God came down that day and set us free from our own unforgiving hearts.

—∽∽∽—

Lord, only You can change the bondage of unforgiveness to the freedom of forgiving. Please put true forgiveness in my heart today.

Karen Porter's work includes: *Bible Seeds* and *Bible Seeds For Enriching Your Character.* Her work has appeared in *Focus on the Family, Godly Business Woman,* and *Discipleship Journal* magazines.

Nest in a Rock

Deborah W. Strubel

Your dwelling place is secure, your nest is set in a rock.

Numbers 24:21 NIV

As a college freshman, I left my goody-goody image at home and aimed to have some fun. I cavorted with rebels and kindred spirits who skated between their Christian upbringing and the ways of the world. In no time at all, I succeeded in making myself miserable.

I hit my lowest point one late October afternoon, as I looked longingly at the Tappan Zee Bridge. A mad dive into the Hudson River would at least end my confusion and pain. Fortunately, it was too far to walk.

Since it was dinnertime on campus and I couldn't face anyone, I hiked to a spot my biology class had visited during an outdoor lab. It was dusk when I reached an opening in the trees at the top of the hill. I wrapped my sweater around me and shivered, surprised at how cold it was after the sun faded. The wind gusted furiously, and I rubbed my arms to stay warm.

Wandering around the large flat rocks that Ice Age glaciers had dropped, I thought they looked like dead, half-buried whales that had beached their whole pod in a final act of togetherness. Suddenly, I felt totally alone.

I was unloved and unlovable. God had surely abandoned me.

I slumped onto the nearest boulder and hung my head. My eyes stung with tears. Wiping my nose on the sleeve of my sweater, I realized I wasn't shivering anymore. I was warm.

I placed my palm on the rock. Its surface radiated warmth that crawled up my fingers, across my wrist, and into my arm. In that instant, I knew God and His love were in the heat of that boulder. He sent that boulder on a mission eons ago so that on a dark windy fall evening I would find Him again in the nest of a warm rock.

⸙

Lord, Thank You that my dwelling is secure, although
I sometimes feel alone. Remind me that You
have a nest for me in the rock of Your love.

Deb Strubel is associate agent with BigScore Productions literary agency, senior editor at Starburst Publishers, and the coauthor of *Single, Whole, and Holy: Christian Women and Sexuality* (Christian Publications, 1996.)

Wherever the
Wind Blows

Janet   Chester   Bly

*In speaking of the angels he says, He makes
his angels winds, his servants flames of fire.*

Hebrews 1:7 NIV

A friend and I determined to pray together for the village and
church where we first met. Both drawn to Winchester, Idaho,
from large California towns, we sensed a spiritual purpose. With
only three hundred citizens for whom to intercede, we anticipated quick, dramatic results.

Seven years passed. We grew in our friendship. We wit-
nessed answers to prayer for our families, but little results
beyond that. Our church still struggled with its small crew of
members. And the city pretty much ignored God while we
wrestled with discouragement.

One Sunday morning, as I helped with the worship team, the
entry door at the back of the church swung open. Must be the
wind, I thought. Then a rush followed. A distinct impression

blew over me that a being had entered, on the order of a powerful warrior angel. For a moment I marveled at the awareness of an awesome presence in the room. But soon I began to chide myself as a frail, gray-haired woman with cane approached aided by a half-dozen strangers. My imagination surely had deceived me.

After the service, I talked to one of the men with the elderly woman. "We attended a family reunion yesterday," he explained. "Grandma insisted we bring her here to church. She found Jesus in this place as a youth. Her family moved away soon after, but she never forgot this sanctuary. And she's become one mighty intercessor. She's prayed every one of us into the kingdom. And lately she says she's been praying for this little church."

I looked at the woman with wonder. Maybe an angel really did come to visit. This event encouraged my friend and me. We prayed with renewed fervor. And soon after, our church began to grow one person, one couple, one family at a time.

Father, guide me to my place, for Your purpose. Direct me to my appointed tasks in this city. Help me persevere when I falter. Send the angel of Your choice to encourage me.

Janet Chester Bly has authored ten books, including *Hope Lives Here,* and coauthored with her husband, Stephen, eighteen books, such as *The Power of a Godly Grandparent.*

How I Really Got My Name

Virelle Kidder

The LORD your God is with you . . . He will quiet you
with His love, He will rejoice over you with singing.

Zephaniah 3:17 NIV

When asked how I got my name, my rote reply has been, "My parents put their names together on the way to the hospital, Virginia and Russell, and out came Virelle!" I never questioned what my mother had told me until I heard God speak to me.

Virelle! came His whisper.

"Is that You, Lord?" I answered, suddenly wide-awake.

I thought you'd like to know how you really got your name. You were wrong, you know.

"But, my mother always told me . . . "

I know, He replied. *That's what she understood at the time. But actually I named you.*

"You did?" The thought had never before occurred to me. I was speechless, stunned to realize anew that God had planned me long before my parents did.

I named you that because I love you. I have always loved you with an everlasting love.

His words brought tears, and with them, release. Like many, I never felt lovable. I knew God loved me, but it seemed like a general love, a blanket covering all His children. With too many things I didn't love about myself, I held back fully believing God's love, until this night.

What happened next rocked my whole world. I lay quietly, listening to my heavenly Father tell me how much He loved me. The verses I have known and loved in His Word, He now whispered to me. When He finished, this happy child fell fast asleep, nestled in the love I now believed was for me too.

———

Father, thank You for loving me so much.
Open my heart to trust Your love with everything
that concerns me today. In Jesus' name, Amen.

Virelle Kidder is the author of several books, a conference speaker, broadcaster, and a contributing writer for *Today's Christian Woman* who lives in upstate New York.

God, My Nightlight

Susan B. Wilson

*Let all who take refuge in you be glad; let them
ever sing for joy. Spread your protection over them
that those who love your name may rejoice in you.*

Psalm 5:11 NIV

*F*ear was my constant companion for years. Checking under beds
and looking in closets, I was convinced that if something terrible was going to happen, it would happen to me.

From the time I left graduate school and lived on my own, I
slept with a light on, clutching a teddy bear with one hand,
leaving my other hand free to grab a pair of scissors from under
the pillow if needed.

Four years later, I married. I felt protected. I felt relief.

I put away the teddy bear and the scissors. It felt safe to turn
out the light. That is, until my husband's first business trip. As
the sun dipped below the horizon, fear crept in as I realized that
I had to endure the night alone.

Despite my love for God, my fear seemed greater than my Father's protection. I suffered repeatedly when Doug had to be gone. There were nights I stayed with friends because I couldn't face a night alone in our home.

Then a baby arrived and two years later, a second. Praise God. I no longer had to be alone in the house. But fear still gnawed at me. When Doug was gone, growing fear accompanied the increasing darkness of each night. And in that darkness, my fear fueled tension and impatience with the children. It also fueled restless nights and active panic.

One night, after waking up with a feeling of terror, I got up, picked up my Bible, and turned to Psalms. After reading for a few minutes, I prayed for God to take my fear and bind it. I prayed for God's protection to be wrapped around me. Peace arrived. I closed my Bible, set it down, and went to sleep.

The peace of God's night-light has freed me for the past six years.

—ᴏᴇᴏ—

Abba, I thank You for the fatherly comfort and protection
You so richly provide, for peace that passes all understanding
as I know that You are my refuge and joy.

Susan Best Wilson is an author, speaker, and expert facilitator. She has authored, coauthored, and/or contributed to seven books, three audio programs, and a video series.

A Beacon of Light

Susan Titus Osborn

Let your light shine before men, that they may see
your good deeds and praise your Father in heaven.

Matthew 5:16 NIV

Shivering, I zipped my windbreaker tightly around my neck and
walked faster along the shore. The damp air chilled me as I
watched the fog roll in. Darkness quickly settled in, but I felt
determined to take my nightly walk. This was my quiet time.

I carefully picked my way across the rocky portion of the
beach to the sandy stretch. In the distance, I saw the beacon
from the lighthouse on the point. I used its flashing light to
guide me.

I thought of how often my life revolved like that beacon, so
busy and yet seeming to go nowhere. I often felt stress from the
many demands on my time. Running an editorial business,
meeting book deadlines, and fitting in speaking engagements
made life a constant juggling act.

I prayed, "Lord, am I doing what you have called me to do? I'm so busy running from one deadline to the next that I lose sight of my purpose."

As I walked toward the lighthouse, the Lord brought to mind a woman who had called me that day. She had purchased one of my writing books and said, "You have no idea how much this book helped me format my picture book."

Then I thought of a single mom who had recently come to me at a conference. She held up my book, *Rest Stops for Single Moms*. With tears in her eyes, she said, "I had no idea anyone knew how I felt."

Finally, I reached the lighthouse and lingered for a moment, gazing at the powerful light. Grasping its awesome responsibility, I realized my own. The Lord wanted me to continue writing so that my words could help those who cross my path.

***

Dear Lord, help me to reach out to those around me with Your love. Please allow me to be a beacon, reflecting Your light.

Susan Titus Osborn is director of the Christian Communicator Manuscript Critique Service, contributing editor of *The Christian Communicator* magazine, and an adjunct professor. She has authored twenty-seven books.

Better Than Apple Pie

Kari West

Keep me as the apple of your eye.

Psalm 17:8 NIV

Twelve years ago, with dreams of apple pie, I carved a hole in the hard clay of my country garden. I pounded a stake and tied a one-gallon tree to it with a strip of insulated wire. Over time, the tree continued to grow over and around the restrictive wire. While cultivating a vegetable patch and picking flowers, I often paused to ooh! and ah! at the apple blossoms with an eye toward harvest, hoping to pick fruit before the raccoon got to it.

Before the tree finally succumbed to fire blight and marauding gophers, all that was visible of the wire was an inch-wide scar ringing the trunk. I couldn't push the wire in or pull it out. The tree had simply learned to live with it, grown beyond it, become fruitful in spite of it.

Recently, I planted a dwarf orange tree in its place. Hacking away the dead limbs and stump of the apple tree, I sensed God slowing me down to show me something. After settling my bottom down in the dirt, I paused to touch the wire—and then, I knew. I was growing around and over life's "if onlys" just the way my apple tree had. Somehow, one season at a time, I grew above the hampering wire of betrayal and loss.

As I caressed the disfigured trunk with my fingertips, I realized that etched in my memories are not only painful situations but also God's presence with me in them and His comfort through them. In that moment, when I finally saw my scars not as fatal flaws but sacred evidence of what I've been through, I felt God reminding me that I am the apple of His eye, uniquely created and divinely gifted for His purpose. My worth isn't tied to a perfect set of circumstances, just as a tree's growth isn't measured by the number of pies.

Lord, grant me grace to adapt to any situation and
teach me to accept the unique person You created me to be.

Kari West, author of *Dare to Trust, Dare to Hope Again: Living with Losses of the Heart*
lives in California with her husband, two dogs, and a goat named Sigmund.

The Power of His Presence

Louise   Tucker   Jones

*The angel of the LORD came back a second time and touched him
and said, "Get up and eat, for the journey is too much for you."*

1 Kings 19:7 NIV

had lost count of how many days and nights it had been
since I slept. Before bringing my young son to the hospital, I sat
in the middle of the bed all night, holding him upright, just to
help him breathe. At the hospital, I kept watch beside Jay's
bed, even crawling into the oxygen tent and cuddling him into
my arms while praying that he would survive. But how many
days and nights, I didn't know. Thankfully, the crisis passed,
and Jay responded to treatment.

Not trusting myself to drive with such fatigue, a friend
picked me up at the hospital and took me home for some
much-needed rest. I fell into bed and sank into oblivion. After

a couple of hours, I awoke. I needed a bath and food, but I was too exhausted to get up. I knew my friend would be back soon to pick me up, but I couldn't get out of bed.

Suddenly, I felt a prompting. *Get up and eat.*

I opened my eyes. I knew no one was in the room, but I could feel God's presence. In my mind, I saw Jesus standing beside my bed, his hand outstretched. *Get up and eat,* He repeated.

"I can't," I answered.

Get up and eat! the gentle voice said again. At that, I fought my way to full consciousness and dragged myself out of bed and into the kitchen where I fixed a can of soup, sensing His pres-ence with me at all times. Not surprisingly, the hot liquid strengthened me immediately. I took a bath. I was dressed and fully rested when my friend picked me up.

I returned to the hospital with a renewed spirit, knowing all would be well with my child and me.

Lord Jesus, just as I held my son so tenderly throughout
his illness, thank You for holding me in my time of need.
May others feel Your presence and glory. Amen.

Louise Tucker Jones is a Gold Medallion Award winning author and inspirational speaker. Married to Carl for thirty-eight years and mother of four, Louise resides in Edmond, Oklahoma.

Astonished by Love

Sherrie Eldridge

*I pray that you, being rooted and established in love, may have
power, together with all the saints, to grasp how wide and long and
high and deep is the love of Christ . . . that surpasses knowledge—
that you may be filled to the measure of all the fullness of God.*

Ephesians 3:17-19 NIV

"Mom," my pregnant daughter, Chrissie, sobbed over the
phone. "The doctors said that the twins are small and have a
rare condition that will surely end in death. One of the doctors
said that he had just heard a pioneering physician from
Milwaukee who does surgery in the womb on babies with this
condition. Do you think we should look into it?"

Within hours, the entire family was in Milwaukee standing
vigil around Chrissie's bed, praying for the best. The chances for
the babies' survival were slim. Both or one of the twins might die,
and they both ran the risk of retardation or multiple sclerosis.

After ten days in the hospital, Chrissie was ordered to strict
bed rest for the remaining three months of her pregnancy.

During that time, she and her husband, Michael, stayed at our home. What a precious time I had with my daughter as we passed the days together, looking at old photos and talking heart to heart.

None of us said it, but we were all afraid of a sad outcome.

Then the day finally came! Two healthy baby boys, Austin and Blake, were born.

I'll never forget the first time I cuddled them in my arms. I looked into their sweet faces and thought, "Little baby, you don't have to do *one thing* to make me love you. I adore you just because of who you are."

Within seconds it was as if someone was standing beside me whispering in my ear, *Sherrie, that's exactly how I feel about you! You don't have to do a thing to prove your worth to me. I adore you just because you are mine.*

I knew it had to be Him!

Lord, thank You for making Your great love real to me.
Please make me a vessel through which
You can pour Your love to others. Amen!

Sherrie Eldridge is the founder and president of Jewel Among Jewels Adoption Network, Inc. She is the author of the highly acclaimed *Twenty Things Adopted Kids Wish Their Adoptive Parents Knew.*

The Touch of His Love

*Praise the LORD, for he has shown me his unfailing love.
He kept me safe when my city was under attack. In sudden
fear I had cried out, "I have been cut off from the LORD!"
But you heard my cry for mercy and answered my call for help.*

Psalm 31:21-22 NLT

*T*hrough the darkest hours of the night, I lay in my bed sobbing.
It had been months since my husband left home. All hope of
his return was gone. I had no strength left to pray. I had no
strength left to wait for a new day to come. I had no strength
left to go on.

The strange calmness of the night made time stand still.
Unanswerable questions rushed through my mind as I lay flat
on my back staring into the darkness. *How can I survive without
my husband at my side? How will my sons become men of God?
Who will take care of us? How could God allow this? Why doesn't
He answer my prayers?*

I rolled over forcing my face into a stack of pillows. Beating my fists on the mattress, I hoped the next breath would be my last. Desperately needing solace, but not wanting to turn to the one who I felt had betrayed me, I finally shouted, "Where are You, God? Why did You leave me too?" Not once, but again and again, until I had no voice left.

As I trusted that tomorrow would not come, I felt the pressure of an arm reach across the small of my back. I could feel the warmth of His presence as if I was being coddled like an infant. My breathing began to deepen; the stream of tears began to subside. He answered my cry for help with the intimacy of His touch.

I had not slept peacefully since the night of my husband's departure. From that night forward, I found the strength to face the uncertainties of each new day with the comfort of being nestled in God's arms at night.

Oh, Father, thank You for Your unfailing love.
You have replaced the pain of rejection with the joy
of being loved by You. To know You is my greatest joy.

Jill McDonald Rigby is the author of *Manners of the Heart*, a manners and etiquette curriculum for elementary schools. She is a sought after speaker with her seminar, *Raising Respectful Children in a Disrespectful World*. Jill is the proud mother of identical twins, twenty-one-year-olds, Boyce and Chad.

You Can Count on It!

Christine   Harder   Tangvald

This is what He promised us—even eternal life.

1 John 2:25 NIV

*O*n June 10, 1985—my forty-fourth birthday—the telephone rang. It was a parent's worst fear. Our second son, Thor, twenty, had fallen earlier in the day in a hiking accident.

The next few moments were a blur.

"So sorry . . . he was killed . . . "

What do you mean? How can this be? No, this is impossible!
Thor is one of the good guys—a God's kid from day one!

"What funeral parlor do you want to "handle things?"

Who will call his brother at college?

Me? What will I say?

Chaos. Internal. External. Emotional. Spiritual. Intellectual. All in chaos. Grief. Loneliness. Panic. Anger. Disbelief. Numbness.

And yet—from the very second of realization that my precious son had died, I had a strong, rock-like sense of peace.

Underneath all the other emotions stood a heavy-duty cable of the presence and reality of God!

God—real, there, present, personal, all I needed.

I lost my precious Son too. And because of My Son, your son instantly experienced eternal life.

A promise I could count on!

Did I cry? Oh, you bet. Sometimes I sobbed so hard I thought I might actually choke to death! I call them "paper towel" cries because tissue just didn't cut it. But, I know and believe with all my heart that, because of God's son, Jesus, my Thor waits for me at the very end of my own time line here on this earth. There he stands—as alive as can be—grinning at me and cheering me on!

"Go, Mom!" he yells. "Live your life with gusto! I'm fine. Don't worry about me. God took great care to see that I am here—waiting for you!"

God's promise is God's presence.

You can count on it!

—∞—

Thank You, God, for allowing Your Son to die for my son.
Oh! And will You please tell my Thor to wait for me.
I'm coming—wait for me!

Christine Harder Tangvald is the author of eighty-five picture books with more than 2.7 million books in print. She, her husband, three children, and eight grandchildren, all live in Spokane, Washington.

Your Treasures Are in His Hand

Jan Frank

Let them know that it is your hand, that you, O LORD, have done it.

Psalm 109:27 NIV

*S*everal years ago, I had a speaking engagement a four-hour drive from my home. The morning I left, it was pouring rain. The weather paralleled my inner storm.

My oldest daughter, Heather, was sixteen. Turmoil filled our home, and my heart ached as I called out Heather's name to God. I arrived, grateful no one was there to meet me. I sat alone in a restaurant with swollen eyes and a heavy heart.

I left the engagement the following morning, dreading the drive home.

An hour into the drive, the sky cleared. To the right, the ocean's water glistened with the sun while trees swayed in the ocean breeze. On the left, everything was still. I couldn't under-stand how this was possible.

You often look for evidence of My working, but it is not always visible to the eye.

I knew the Lord was speaking about Heather.

"Lord, I can't see any evidence, and I'm broken-hearted."

Jan, everything that you hold precious, I hold in My hand. Heather is in My hand, and you can trust Me. The sun's warmth flooded me with God's peace.

I told no one, but held onto His promise. Nine months later, a friend, who'd known nothing of the turmoil, handed me a gift: a piece of silver with a hand clutching a handbag. I looked puzzled and asked what it meant. She said, "A few months ago, the Lord said, *Buy that for Jan.* He told me to tell you that every-thing you hold precious, He holds in His hand." I burst into tears, reminded once again that He is faithful to His promises.

⌇

Lord, thank You for Your faithfulness. Thank You that
You promise to complete the good work You have begun.
I trust You with all that is precious to me.

Jan Frank is the author of *Door of Hope* (Nelson) and coauthor of
Unclaimed Baggage (Nav Press). She is a conference speaker
and resides in California with her husband, Don.

Above and Beyond

Debi Stack

Some trust in chariots and some in horses,
but we trust in the name of the LORD our God.

Psalm 20:7 NIV

*J*okes, weather, recipes. Conspiracy alerts, prayer requests, travel deals. Nothing unusual about that day's e-mail—until the final mouse click opened a message that sent me reeling.

The deadline for my book on perfectionism was weeks away, and I'd been writing with the assumption that its topic was not overdone. Then I read the e-mail announcement that another Christian woman author—one I'd met, liked, read, and admired—was also writing a book on perfectionism. She had numerous books, a website, a whirlwind speaking ministry, and stories from some of the biggest names in the industry for her book on my topic.

I'm not sure which sank lower, my jaw or my heart. I wanted to run away.

Wrapped in misery and wool, I headed into the nippy winter air to walk, think, and pray. My fears tumbled out: *Lord, she's already famous! Her book's release date is before mine! She has celebrities' stories! Why did You lead me to write this book if You knew she was going to do the same thing first?*

His voice in my heart asked, *Whom do you trust?*

Psalm 20:7 came to mind, and immediately my spirits lifted and my stride quickened to this paraphrased cadence: Some trust in agents, but I trust in the name of the Lord my God! Some trust in editors, but I trust in the name of the Lord my God!

I knew He wanted me to complete the book simply out of focused obedience to Him, even if He would be the only One to ever read the finished product.

As for the other woman, she not only endorsed my book, but a year later, she asked me to endorse a new one of hers. Only a trustworthy and generous God could accomplish that.

⊸⊶

Lord, protect me from trusting in anything but Your all-powerful name for every detail of what You've called me to do. Increase my unconditional trust and contentment in You alone.

Debi Stack is a popular speaker whose humorous, self-help book for "maxed out" women, *Martha to the Max: Balanced Living for Perfectionists* (Moody Press), is in multiple printings and translations.

God and the Wind

Teresa Bell Kindred

The wind blows wherever it pleases. You hear its sound,
but you cannot tell where it comes from or where
it is going. So it is with everyone born of the Spirit.

John 3:8 NIV

When our twin boys were about eight years old, they went through a "wiggle phase" at church. It was next to impossible to keep them still. My husband and I talked to them many times about the importance of listening during worship, but it seemed like they weren't getting anything out of the service—at least that's what I thought.

Then on one very windy day, the boys and I were driving down a road lined with trees on both sides. The wind was so strong that the force bent the trees. Leaves skittered and danced their way across the highway. Suddenly Grant asked me one of those questions that I wasn't sure how to answer.

"Mama, why can't we see the wind?"

As I pondered how best to answer his question, Russell, his older brother by four minutes, said, "I know! The wind is like God. We can't see the wind, but we know it's there because we see it moving the trees. We can't see God, but we know He's there because we can see the things that He does."

I was speechless. At that moment, I felt God's love for my boys and me pouring over us like warm sunshine on a cool and cloudy day. I had wanted to plant the seed, water it, and see instant fruit, but that's not the way God works. In that moment God revealed to me that by taking them to Sunday school class, worship, vacation Bible school, and other church-related events, I was planting seed. But just as a seed doesn't grow into a tree overnight, a little boy doesn't grow into a man of faith all at once. With time, a good dose of watering by the Word, the warmth of God's love, and mama's and daddy's prayers, that faith will grow.

—⚬⚬⚬—

God, increase my faith and wisdom that I might better
serve You, remembering You love my children and want
them to grow in faith just as much as I do. Amen.

Teresa Bell Kindred is a wife, mother, freelance writer, author of four *Precious Moments* gift books, columnist for *Kentucky Living* magazine, and public speaker.

Peace Before the Storm

Bonnie Keen

~

"The Lord God is my Strength, my personal bravery,
and my invincible army; He makes my feet like hind's feet
and will make me to walk [not to stand still in terror,
but to walk] and make [spiritual] progress upon my
high places [of trouble, suffering or responsibility]!"

Habakkuk 3:19 AMP

In 1993, Contemporary Christian Music (CCM) recording trio, First Call, was invited to tour with a high profile artist. Coinciding with our biggest recording contract and a season of new dreams, we were thrilled.

Ironically, on this tour, our ministry broke apart.

Years earlier, I had gone through an unwanted divorce. Single parenthood and many a tear-filled night were woven into the tapestry of my private life. By contrast, the group, First Call, seemed immune to disaster.

While on tour, I noticed unsettling choices of behavior in those around me. After the last concert, an affair between one of our members with the leading artist hit the news. Shipwrecked marriages landed First Call in a frenzy of publicity—our picture in *The National Enquirer!*

God knew what was coming—the tidal wave of an impending storm that would wash away ten years of work and friendships. It was enough to lead me into a clinical depression.

Yet before the thunder rolled came three words of hope.

Near the end of the tour, I found myself alone on an oceanfront, wooden walkway. An Eden-like sense saturated the green foliage, flowers, and beauty around me. My heavy heart lifted that morning with the pure medicine of peace. I praised God for simple sounds like waves hitting the shore and a rare experience of joy.

Suddenly I heard three words pressed into my mind: *Do not fear.* I began to weep. Afraid of what? I didn't know. But God was telling me He would be with me in the weeks ahead. It was as if He'd swooped me up into His arms, smiling into my soul.

Those words saw me through much loss and agony. *Do not fear* covered the years of healing that followed. How lovingly the Lord prepared me for His unfailing comfort.

Holy Father, as You go before, walk beside, and follow behind my every circumstance, the intimacy of Your faithful care speaks eternal hope to my heart. Soli deo gloria, Amen!

Bonnie Keen, author of *Blessed Are the Desperate* and *God Loves Messy People,* (Harvest House Publishers), also has two solo recorded projects. She presently travels as a speaker and singer.

From Darkness to Light

Sherrie Eldridge

❦

*I will lead the blind by ways they have not known, along
unfamiliar paths I will guide them; I will turn the darkness
into light before them and make the rough places smooth.*

Isaiah 42:16 NIV

I'm a fairly seasoned traveler but have always dreaded the
prospect of going through a New York airport. What if I got
lost? What if I missed my plane?

Those thoughts flooded my soul when I left for a trip to tape
a television interview in New York. The plan was to leave in
the morning and come home the same evening.

But just before the taping, power was lost, and I ended up
stranded for three days in New York during the largest blackout
in U.S. history, with only a purse and cell phone to my name.

I can't begin to tell how God tenderly cared for me during those dark hours. For example, God's provision included lodging when thousands were on the street; an opportunity to share the gospel with the limo driver; my much-needed medications provided through a stranger I "happened" to meet, who shared her prescription with me; the gift of a bottle of fresh water when I was penniless; peace of mind when riding with a cab driver who couldn't speak English; and my own eager anticipation of what surprise He would provide next.

His presence was so real as I prayed and meditated repeatedly on Psalm ninety-one that I had assurance that His angels were holding me up.

Without question, I knew I had experienced God's tender care in a rather desperate time. If you had told me prior to leaving for New York that one of my deepest fears could be transformed into one of the brightest moments, I would have laughed. But through my encounter with God, that's exactly what happened. He met me in my time of need.

As long as I have breath, I want to declare Your tender mercies and faithfulness to me, Lord. I can't keep quiet!

Sherrie Eldridge is the author of *Twenty Things Adopted Kids Wish Their Adoptive Parents Knew* and *Twenty Life-Transforming Choices Adoptees Need to Make.*

Hope Blooms

Lynn D. Morrissey

Find rest, O my soul, in God alone; my hope comes from him.

Psalm 62:5 NIV

In the dead of winter, my beloved aunt Martha was dying of cancer. My hope, like an ugly amaryllis bulb which I'd planted in a flowerpot on the kitchen windowsill, lay buried beneath ugly fears. *Where was God?*

The closer Martha came to death, the more I feared for her salvation. Whenever I prayed, she pushed me away urging, "Stop, honey. You're scaring me."

Then one day at the nursing home, I sensed God's presence. *Ask her why she's afraid,* He prompted. Finally her anguish spilled out. "You pray because you think I'm going to die. Lynn, I'm so afraid of dying!" How relieved I was to explain that there was nothing to fear if she knew Christ. My joy overflowed as Aunt Martha asked to receive Jesus as her Savior.

When I got home, I stopped to linger at the kitchen window, mesmerized by emerald amaryllis shoots towering two feet over the flowerpot. In just weeks since I'd planted the bulb, I'd watched in amazement at the leaves' skyrocketing growth. I was most eager to see the bright red blooms promised by the potting instructions. Despite the devastation of death surrounding me, the amaryllis had become an undeniable symbol of life and hope.

That evening, we got the call that Martha had died. I felt lifeless and couldn't cry. The morning of the funeral, as I filled the teakettle at the kitchen sink, I was incredulous! Amazingly, I beheld three brilliant crimson blossoms uplifted and open wide. The amaryllis "trumpets" had bloomed simultaneously, pointing toward heaven—gloriously heralding my aunt's homecoming. To me, they symbolized the Father, Son, and Holy Spirit, welcoming her in love. I have never felt God's presence more palpably. Finally, tears flowed—tears of gratitude, tears of joy.

Lord, help me to remember that though I don't always sense
Your nearness, You are here, working in miraculous ways
to bring hope from fear and life from death.

Lynn D. Morrissey is an inspirational CLASS speaker and author of
Seasons of a Woman's Heart and her upcoming "passion" book,
Love Letters to God (Multnomah Publishers, January 2004).

His Tender Care through Tragedy

Karol Ladd

Do not fear, for I am with you; do not be dismayed
for I am your God. I will strengthen you and help you;
I will uphold you with my righteous right hand.

Isaiah 41:10 NIV

*T*he phone rang in the early morning hours. A friend called to
inform me that a car had hit my mother during her daily walk.
I was startled. *How could a healthy, alert, fifty-five-year-old*
woman be hit while walking in her quiet neighborhood? I arrived at
the scene of the accident only to find she'd been rushed to the
trauma unit downtown. I began to pray for help and comfort for
Mom, as well as assistance for me to get to the hospital.

"Please let it be him," I whispered seeing a car in rush hour
traffic that looked like my husband's. Miraculously it was! At
the sound of my horn, he pulled over, and we sped away
together in his car. Grabbing his Bible from the backseat, I

began searching for comforting verses. Oddly, every verse I read spoke of the glory of entering Heaven. I kept looking for healing verses, but God only allowed me to find heavenly verses. To this point, I'd not considered death a possibility. I was worried that mother was hurt, but death on a neighborhood street? No way!

My voice quivered, "I think God is trying to tell me that Mom has died." I could feel inside that what I said was true. God was lovingly, tenderly preparing my heart for the news. Arriving at the hospital, we were told of her death, yet God had already given us His peace in the knowledge that she was in His presence.

Reports rolled in, telling of a silver-haired man who mercifully cared for my mom during her dying moments on the street. We never found the man to thank him, but some say he was an angel; others think he was a local doctor. Whoever he was, he was God's loving provision for my mother as she was ushered to her eternal home.

Most gracious and loving Lord, thank You for Your wisdom,
care, and unfailing love. It's wonderful to know that
You're at work in the smallest details of my life.

Karol Ladd is a popular speaker and the author of fourteen books including
Power of a Positive Mom, Table Talk, and *Scream Savers.*

The Voice from out of the Rock

Sharon Hoffman

We do not know what to do, but our eyes are upon you.

2 Chronicles 20:12 NIV

*B*oth believers since childhood, my husband Rob and I studied the Bible, taught it, and prayed for God's will in our lives. Rob led our church as senior pastor, and he whole-heartedly supported my ministry of writing and speaking. We'd traveled a path together that should have led to contentment, a life that would bring fulfillment and satisfaction.

Even so, something was missing. Nagging questions and an unexplained emptiness kept our spirits restless. Often I prayed, "Father, show us just what it is You want us to do. We'll do it!" Overwhelmed with anxiety and a little frightened of being moved out of our comfort zone, we sought counsel from the Lord at a lovely lodge in the serene, marble mountains of Colorado.

On a long, solitary prayer walk late one afternoon, though not audible, God's answer to me was loud and clear. Who, but God, would stop me in my tracks to notice a single wild flower growing, of all places, out of the top of a large boulder? It seemed as strange to me as a burning bush must have seemed to Moses. I thought my eyes were betraying me. Flowers grow in soil; they don't grow in rock.

But this one did.

"Make us bloom brightly and beautifully, Lord, even if you take us to hard places." Deep inside I could sense that He had heard my prayer.

Within a year, God led Rob and me to a triumphant, new ministry. He has held our hands every step of the way and has never let go. When I show friends and family our memory album of Colorado, I always start with the picture of my flower in the rock. It has been a message of joy and hope to many.

———

Precious Lord, thank You for the beauty that grows from
the hard places. Teach me daily to trust You with my life,
knowing You have the best of plans for me.

Sharon Hoffman speaks at women's conferences worldwide and
is the author of five books and founder of GIFTed Living Ministries.
She and her pastor-husband, Rob, live in North Carolina.

Timing Is Everything

Martha Bolton

*Trust in the LORD with all your heart and
lean not on your own understanding.*

Proverbs 3:5 NIV

When our two-year-old son was scheduled to undergo the first of two major heart surgeries, my husband and I drove him to the hospital, filled out the admission papers, and waited for the pre-op examination to begin. Even knowing that we had one of the best pediatric cardiologists and a leading heart surgeon on the case didn't make it any easier. We had to lean on God.

The surgery was canceled and later rescheduled because the pre-op exam revealed that our son had a slight elevation in body temperature. This scheduling and rescheduling went on for several weeks, and I finally had a talk with God about it. I told Him that I would certainly prefer that our son didn't have to go through these surgeries at all, but if he did, then I wanted to get them behind us.

Our timing isn't always God's timing. The surgery was scheduled again; and once again it had to be postponed.

"God, didn't you hear my prayer?" I asked. I didn't understand why we had to endure this emotional roller coaster.

But God had heard my prayers. God in his silence, just wanted me to trust him.

That next week I received my answer. A spokesman for the hospital was on the news explaining that one of their pediatric physicians had been diagnosed with hepatitis. The hospital stated that any children who had been seen by this physician should return to the hospital for testing and, if necessary, treatment. Since my son had only been seen by a nurse and discharged each time, he hadn't been exposed. God had protected our son from a danger we didn't even know existed.

The surgeries were later performed, and everything went well—in God's perfect timing. Not mine.

─── ∞ ───

Lord, thank You for being Someone I can trust every
hour of every day in whatever circumstances.
You see the whole picture when I cannot.

Martha Bolton is an Emmy-nominated and Dove-nominated writer. She is the author of more than fifty books of humor and inspiration.

Communion among the Redwoods

Karen Porter

*In him we have redemption through his blood, the forgiveness
of sins, in accordance with the riches of God's grace that
he lavished on us with all wisdom and understanding.*

Ephesians 1:7-8 NIV

*E*normous redwoods surround the lodges and meeting rooms of
Mt. Hermon Conference Center. On Palm Sunday, fog gave way
to sunshine as dual pianos beckoned the crowd to the sanctuary.

Poetic words flowed. *Hosanna!* Descriptions of the king
riding on a mere donkey. Thoughts of Mary—how her hand-
maiden's joyous heart became a mother's broken heart only to
return to a joyous heart again. Oh, the wondrous cross!

The minister spoke of Jesus' broken body as he held up the
loaf. Unexpectedly, tears filled my eyes when he tore the bread
in two and I caught a glimpse of Jesus' indescribable pain. We
each held our small portion of bread until all were served,
sharing in the moment just as we all share in His body.

When we received our tiny cups, the minister said, "To symbolize our individual decisions to follow Christ, please drink from your cup when you are ready."

Always before, the minister instructed the audience to drink in unison. It was a ceremony. Familiar. We usually repeated Jesus' words, *"Remember Me"* before we drank.

Now he asked me to make it personal. To take the cup when *I* was ready. My mind whirled. How would I ever be ready? How could I share in His blood?

My hand shook, the little cup almost spilling. I felt alone. Me and the cup.

Then I felt the Savior's presence as if He were sitting next to me. *This cup is the new covenant in my blood which is poured out for you. Whoever eats my flesh and drinks my blood has eternal life.*

Trembling, I lifted the cup to my lips. Jesus whispered, *I'm in my Father, and you're in me and I'm in you,* as I experienced sweet communion under the wings of giant redwoods.

Thank You Father for the plan of salvation. Thank You Jesus for carrying out the plan flawlessly. Thank You for Your sacrifice. Thank You for the joy of communion.

Karen Porter's work includes: Bible Seeds and Bible Seeds For Enriching Your Character. Her work has appeared in Focus on the Family, Godly Business Woman, and Discipleship Journal magazines.

Committed to the Journey

Peg Carmack Short

*Don't ask me to leave you and turn back. I will go wherever
you go, and live wherever you live. Your people will be my
people, and your God will be my God. I will die where you
die and will be buried there. May the LORD punish me
severely if I allow anything but death to separate us!*

Ruth 1:16-17 NLT

J awake to the aroma of freshly brewed coffee, my favorite
way to start the day. My husband gets up first and prepares it as
a little gift of love. After thirty-eight years of marriage, we
know the ritual well. We'll sit and talk before the whirling
dervish of life intrudes on our day.

I have known and loved this man most of my life, but it has
not always been one happy ever after. Fifteen years ago, an
accident threatened to change our lives forever. My husband,
Bob, was on a business trip in San Francisco. I returned home
to a message saying, "Bob's been in an accident. Call the emergency room immediately and speak to the neurosurgeon."

The call confirmed my worst fears. Bob had a severe brain injury. He required immediate surgery. The prognosis: possibly death, or if he survived, probable loss of speech and the use of the right side of his body.

As I flew to his side, I prayed. Almost unable to form coherent words, I plead, "Lord, please help us." Then I heard an audible voice say, "All is well." Instantly I went from a racing heart to complete peace knowing these words were the voice of God.

For the next few days, I stayed constantly by Bob's bedside. But his condition worsened. A second emergency surgery was required. After that, a miracle occurred. His intellect, personality, and body functions were intact. Though the coming weeks and months were filled with both health and financial challenges, we faced these difficulties together through prayer and love.

Through this difficulty, we have learned to cherish every day, every gentle word, and each act of kindness. We understand that love and life are wonderful God-given gifts. We have persevered because of our *commitment* to the words: "I will go wherever you go . . . and only death will separate us."

―∞―

Lord, help us to love one another and to be faithful to our marriage commitment—to walk through life together, whether good times or bad. Let me see and cherish all that is good in my spouse.

Peg Carmack Short both speaks and writes on the importance of marriage and family life. Currently she is writing *A Still Life, Creating Quieting Spaces for Your Home and Heart.*

Never Lost

Victorya Michaels Rogers

O LORD, you have searched me and you know me. You know when I sit and when I rise; you perceive my thoughts from afar. You discern my going out and my lying down; you are familiar with all my ways. Before a word is on my tongue you know it completely, O LORD.

Psalm 139:1-4 NIV

I went home for my Grandma Stella's funeral two years ago. She had lived a wonderful eighty-eight years. While making the arrangements for her memorial, I drove my Grandpa George around in my rental car, which was a blessed distraction for him. This particular rental car had one of those fun new contraptions called a GPS (Global Positioning Satellite). Grandpa had never seen anything like it before.

For two days I took him on various errands while the GPS audibly and visually announced where to turn and how far we had left to go for each new destination. It even told us when we went the wrong way and gave new directions stating how to get back on course. With the GPS, we were never lost!

At dinner with my parents, Grandpa made a profound statement: "It's just amazing to me," he said. "Some little chip in this car is signaling a satellite twenty-five miles in the air, and that satellite knows exactly where we are in the midst of millions of people, even with dozens of cars surrounding us. It even knows when we've made a wrong turn! If a man-made device can know that many details about me, then I finally understand how big God is."

I realized God reached out and met Grandpa in the midst of his grief. With millions of other people in this world, God still cared about Grandpa's pain and knew exactly where he was. I will never forget that moment. What an awesome God we serve! He sees and cares for each of us individually. Every time we rise and every time we lie down, He knows. With God we are never lost.

———

Dear Jesus, thank You for knowing every detail of my life, even with millions of other people around. Guide me today, Lord. Intervene when I'm on the wrong road and show me where to turn. Amen.

Former Hollywood agent Victorya Michaels Rogers coauthored *The Day I Met God* and *How to Talk About Jesus Without Freaking Out.*

A Divine Hug

Kathe Wunnenberg

To Him who is able to do immeasurably more than
all we ask or imagine . . . to Him be glory.
Ephesians 3:20-21 NIV

*G*od often fills our deepest longings in unexpected ways. I encountered God on an ordinary day when I felt as if my world was unraveling. As a forty-something mom to two toddler boys and a teenage son, I'd become so sleep deprived and physically weary that I cried out, "Lord, take me home!"

One morning as I slumped on my couch between my juice-sipping, cookie-crunching toddlers, I wondered how I'd ever make it through the day. If only I lived near family, then I could get a break, I thought. I imagined what it would feel like to have grandparents living next door who would cuddle my children while I took a long hot shower and got dressed. My daydream was cut short by the ring of the phone.

"Kathe, it's Carol," sobbed my friend. "I'm outside in my car. I need a Joshie hug!"

Robe-clad with babe in arms, I hugged my grieving friend whose grandchildren had just moved away. She shared how much she missed her two-year-old grandson, "Joshie," and how God told her to drive to my house.

We shared coffee, conversation, laughter, and tears. Then "Mae Mae Carol" encouraged me to take a break. As I ascended the stairs, I sensed God's presence in a powerful way as I watched my friend giving hugs and tickling toes. Standing in the steaming shower, I was in awe of God's personal love to meet me where I was that very day. Refreshed and dressed, I watched my smiling two-year-old son, Joshua, throw his arms around my friend and say, "Bye, Bye Mae Mae! Come see me again, okay?"

I knew without a doubt that God does give divine hugs, that He is always there, listening—even anticipating—my every need!

***

Your personal love for me amazes me. Thank You for
hugging me through others. Use me to reach out
to someone in need of Your touch today.

Kathe Wunnenberg is a retreat speaker and the author of *Grieving the Loss of a Loved One* and *Grieving the Child I Never Knew*. She lives in Phoenix with her family.

Stand in the Gap

Kathy Blume

*If my people, who are called by my name, will humble
themselves and pray and seek my face and turn from
their wicked ways, then will I hear from heaven and
will forgive their sin and will heal their land.*

2 Chronicles 7:14 NIV

*M*y husband was part of the Promise Keepers team that
orchestrated the gathering of 1.2 million men in the
Washington, DC Mall to declare their faith in God and *Stand
in the Gap* for their families and their nation.

I was privileged to be part of the Intercessory Team that had
prayed for months before the event. Part of our mission was to
"prayer walk" the Mall and every zip code in Washington DC.

Four days before the event, my husband called in a panic
because of the local restrictions, which were not being lifted. I
alerted some of the warriors, and we sought the heart of God.
This is what we heard, *Get all the men on your team out of bed,*

go down to the Mall, and declare that this event is accomplished in the name of Jesus Christ. Walk the Mall, and do nothing but Praise and Worship. They were obedient and did as the Lord asked.

By 10:00 the next morning, during yet another round of negotiations, all of the restrictions were suddenly lifted and resolved.

Early on the morning of the fourth, we walked again to the Mall in anticipation of praying one last time. As we walked onto the Mall, there was an overwhelming feeling of the presence of God. A million men were already in place, and I could still hear myself breathe. God and His glory encompassed us like nothing I'd ever experienced. We had done the work, and now God invited us to simply lay it all down and worship Him.

Men's lives were changed for eternity because of the faithful prayers of those who believed that we serve a God whose plans will not be thwarted by any power on earth or in the heavens.

⸻

Holy God, I bow low in Your presence in awe and humility
that You have chosen to have a relationship with me
and reveal Yourself in such magnificent ways.

Kathy Blume communicates God's incredible healing, restoration, and renewal to Christian campuses and retreats both internationally and in one-on-one mentoring. Her passion is prayer. She has published several articles in various books.

God Loves Me No Matter How I Feel

Cynthia Spell Humbert

I have loved you with an everlasting love;
I have drawn you with loving-kindness.

Jeremiah 31:3 NIV

I think in an all or nothing manner about God. Knowing in my head that God loves me is easy, but always feeling His love in my heart can be difficult. I am like the girl plucking petals from a daisy saying, "He loves me, He loves me not." When I hear about women receiving a word from God, I think, *I guess You have favored children. I have never heard from you that way, so* . . . "He loves me not."

Recently, while teaching at a retreat, I spoke about the brokenness of my own life. I shared how God's love and grace can make a beautiful mosaic when we are willing to give Him control of our broken pieces.

As I closed the session, the worship leader, whom I had not met, approached me and asked me to remain on stage. She said, "Cynthia, God has only asked me to do this one other time. He wants me to sing this song to you from Him."

"My Cynthia, I love you," she sang.

"I know you are mine, for you, all your sins laid on me, God Divine.

"My precious redeemed one, my loved one art thou,

"If ever I loved you, my Cynthia it's now."

As she sang, I stood and wept. I felt the loving embrace of my heavenly Father. Through the song, I heard God clearly say, *Not only do I love you, you belong to Me.* This is the only specific and direct message I have ever had from God. Remembering that day helps me know the truth—we are each special children no matter what our feelings tell us.

———

*Abba Father, thank You that in a world that always changes,
You never change! It is such a peaceful blessing to know
that Your love and faithfulness are constant!
Praise to Your Holy Name Yahweh!*

Cynthia Spell Humbert was a therapist at the Minirth-Meier Clinic in Dallas. She is a national speaker and the author of the NavPress book *Deceived by Shame, Desired by God.*

Eternal Perspective

Sandra Christenson

*For our struggle is not against flesh and blood, but against the
rulers, against the authorities, against the powers of this dark world
and against the spiritual forces of evil in the heavenly realms.*

Ephesians 6:12 NIV

The sun shone through the adjoining dining room windows. I
stood at the kitchen counter, my head laid upon my crossed arms,
tears flowing in evidence of the pain I had for my husband's lack
of relationship with God, with me, and with our children.

The four years of unemployment, the loss of virtually everything material, and the subsequent years of un- and underem-
ployment were nothing compared to the day that I boldly asked
my husband, "Have you been involved with pornography?" The
God-led question slipped from my lips before I had a chance to
deceive myself any longer.

"Yes."

I slammed the phone down.

With ensuing, raging anger, I recollected circumstantial evidence previously dismissed. Pornography was only part of the

truth. My entire marriage was a farce! All that I trusted, all that I gave myself to, all that I believed, was a travesty! *God how could you allow this knowing that I sought Your permission to marry him in the first place?*

Before my rage could fully surface, the scripture "For our struggle is not against flesh and blood, but against the rulers, against the authorities, against the powers of this dark world and against the spiritual forces of evil in the heavenly realms," surged through my mind. It was the Holy Spirit blitzing a message He didn't want me to miss.

Aloud, pressed-lipped and reluctantly, I uttered, "OK, Whatever it takes. God, I'll endure this too."

Little did I know that my prayer would be so difficult to endure. But if I had chosen divorce as an option, today my husband would not be turning back to the Lord, and today my children would not have an intact family.

Lord, thank You for all of it.

—❧—

Lord, sometimes it's hard to see your blessings while I'm hurting. It's hard to make difficult decisions in the midst of trials. But you honor a life lived for you. Thank You for the privilege of doing just that.

Sandra Christenson is an assumed name of a Christian retreat and conference speaker, author, and media personality who is devoted to helping others live not according to the world, but consistent with the transformed life Jesus Christ offers.

Perfect Shells and Broken Pieces

Susan Titus Osborn

Cast all your anxiety on him because he cares for you.

1 Peter 5:7 NIV

I walked along the beach one autumn morning, hoping to find shells. The summer tourists had gone home, so the beach was deserted except for an elderly couple, walking hand-in-hand.

I seemed to be the only person searching for shells, and all I could find were broken pieces. I kicked at the sand in frustration. The broken shells reminded me of the fragmented pieces of my own life since the breakup of my marriage.

The wind whipped my hair and sent a chill down my back, but I pulled my sweatshirt around me and kept walking. Somehow, I hoped my brisk pace would help me leave my problems behind to be swept out with the tide. Instead, the waves kept bringing in more and more broken shells.

I paused and cried out, "Where are you, Lord? What plans do you have for the broken pieces of my life?" I resumed walking, trying to gain some perspective on my situation.

Another wave surged on the shore, and I continued my search. To my surprise, this one brought in a beautiful whole shell. Scooping it up in my hand, I turned it over and noticed how perfectly God had formed it. In the midst of all this brokenness, there was wholeness. I felt a warm peace wash over me, and I realized at that moment that in His time, God would once again make me whole.

Today as I gaze at my perfect shell and think back to a walk on the beach that happened fifteen years ago, I realize how powerfully God spoke to me that day. Although I was a struggling single mom for six years, now I am blessed with a supportive husband and a thriving business. God took the broken pieces of my life and restored me to wholeness.

───

Dear God, please take the broken fragments of my life and make me whole. Please help me not to dwell on the past, but to look to the future, armed with Your presence. Amen.

Susan Titus Osborn is director of the Christian Communicator Manuscript Critique Service, contributing editor of *The Christian Communicator* magazine, and an adjunct professor. She has authored twenty-seven books.

Stretching

Karen   Porter

"My command is this: Love each other as I have loved you.
Greater love has no one than this,
that he lay down his life for his friends."

John 15:12-13 NIV

I was ready to fire her on the spot.

As a manager, hiring and firing is part of the job, but letting an employee go is not the kind of thing I enjoy.

But that day, I was ready. She had stirred up enough trouble in my department to boil a teakettle. And now I was steaming too, especially over the hurtful things she had said about me as well as the chaos she created among the other employees. I'd already cleared the decision with my boss and planned exactly what I would say.

When the woman arrived, I closed the door to my office. The air seemed heavy with tension, but I knew what I had to do. As I walked around my desk to take my seat, my mind flashed back to the previous Sunday night, and a scene played before my eyes.

My pastor was standing before a hostile church meeting about to call for an unpleasant vote. He knew that rumors and accusations about a staff member had spread like wildfire and the vote would probably favor dismissal. As tears filled his eyes, he said, "If you are going to stretch, stretch in the direction of generosity."

And before I opened my mouth to dismiss my employee, I heard the gentle voice of Jesus, whisper, "Stretch, Karen. Stretch."

Then I heard my own voice, "You have a job here for as long as you need one."

That day an encounter with the loving, forgiving, living Lord encouraged me to stretch into mercy and grace. I'm glad I listened, too, because the tension lifted and she worked for me for several more months until she resigned to move to another city. No hard feelings, just stretch marks.

Lord, please teach me to stretch, bend, and even break if necessary so that I can lavish grace, mercy, and peace on others, especially to those who have hurt me.

Karen Porter is a Bible teacher, national speaker, author, and conference leader from Texas.

The Source of My Strength

Deborah Raney

*He said to me, "My grace is sufficient for you, for my power is made
perfect in weakness." Therefore I will boast all the more gladly about
my weaknesses, so that Christ's power may rest on me. That is why,
for Christ's sake, I delight in weaknesses, in insults, in hardships, in
persecutions, in difficulties. For when I am weak, then I am strong.*

2 Corinthians 12:9-10 NIV

*A*t twenty-four I'd never lost anyone dear to me. My grandparents were living, and I was privileged to know one of my
great-grandmothers. I was a strong Christian, learning to walk
ever more closely with the Lord. But one night I told a close
friend that I felt certain that if I ever lost a close family
member—especially if it was someone too young to die—that I
would literally go crazy. I did not believe my faith was strong
enough to see me through such a tragedy.

Two weeks later the phone rang. It was my father, calling to
tell me what seemed unimaginable. My younger sister—so
beautiful and full of life, a newlywed of only three months, and

one semester from fulfilling her dream of being a teacher—had been killed in a car crash.

Though there was a waver in his voice, Daddy encouraged me before he hung up. "Your faith is strong. We'll all get through this with God's help."

I sat there, numb and in shock for several minutes, waiting to come unglued, waiting for my prediction to come true. Waiting to lose my mind.

Instead, sitting there trying to grasp the reality of what had happened, I became aware of a strength I felt well up inside me that I'd never experienced before. God wrapped His arms around me in that moment, and I felt a comfort no human had ever been able to offer me.

In my spirit, I knew this overwhelming peace had nothing to do with me. It was Christ in me, the hope of glory. Since that day, I have never again feared falling apart in the midst of tragedy. I trust that though I am still weak, He is all the strength I will ever need.

⸻

Father God, thank You that my faith doesn't depend on my own strength, but that You supply a reservoir that is replenished when I am weakest, when my need is greatest.

Deborah Raney is the author of several non-fiction books and eight novels, including *A Vow to Cherish,* which was the inspiration for World Wide Pictures' highly acclaimed film of the same title.

Encountering Fear, Encountering God

Joan Esherick

Do not fear, for I am with you.

Isaiah 41:10 NIV

During my childhood, I relished the haven I found at my parents' lakefront cottage. I drifted for hours on end in our old wooden rowboat, while lost in my own imaginary world. I was such a reader back then. Everywhere on the lake's deep waters felt secure to me, except for "the logs."

"The logs" was a section of shoreline that held trees long ago fallen. The water's edge revealed bony trunks, while once-towering evergreens haunted the world beneath the waves. Their skeletal frames, draped with algae and moss, rested just beneath the surface and made an imposing impression on a girl of nine or ten.

My brothers' tales of log monsters didn't help. I had only to recall the clawing of the boat's bottom as I rowed over "the logs" to believe my brothers' stories. Ah—childhood fears.

I'm grown now. Yet, while canoeing over "the logs" last summer, the familiar fear returned. My breathing grew rapid, my palms began to sweat. How silly! There I was, a forty-something woman, fearing the make-believe.

Then God nudged my heart, *You fear what you cannot see, Joan. You fear what lies ahead.* He was right. I faced, and feared, several unknowns—a disabled son starting college, uncertain finances, a parent's declining health, and a national publicity campaign.

But God did more than reveal my fear; He revealed Himself. *I am the God who knows the unknown and sees the unseen,* He reminded me. *I am good, faithful, loving, and upright in all My ways. Your unknown future is not unknown to Me, and I hold you in My hands.*

At His words, my heart stilled. My fear dissolved.

I knew then that my fears were no match for the God who ruled them. God's presence removed my fear.

*O Father, show me "the logs" in my life. Then remind me
of the truth of who You are. Help me to surrender
my fears to You and find rest in Your character.*

Joan Esherick, an author, speaker, and freelance writer, lives in
southeastern Pennsylvania. She continues to offer her
"logs" to the God who reigns and is trustworthy.

Family Embrace

Jan Coleman

Tell it to your children, and let your children tell it to their children, and their children to the next generation.

Joel 1:3 NIV

*W*hen my parents died unexpectedly, my heart burned with regret. I knew they'd met during at a USO dance on Dad's way overseas, but little more. Suddenly they were gone, and tears spilled for the stories I would never hear, the history I could never pass down to my daughters. *Why hadn't they shared more of their lives? Why hadn't I ever asked?*

As a rain drizzled outside, I stood in their empty garage— the last of my clean-up tasks—saying goodbye to them. As I was about to lock the door, my eyes were drawn to a bit of cardboard jutting out from high in the rafters. *Something I'd missed?*

About to toss the tattered box full of old papers, I glanced inside. There were letters, dozens of them, written to my father during World War II, letters from a war familiar to me only in the movies. I dashed into the house and sat on the carpet with my find.

I was captivated by these first-hand accounts of America during a time of uncertainty. My mother chatted on about bond drives, victory gardens, and being a Junior Hostess with the USO: "I'm jitterbugging my way through the war, getting corns for my country. Every soldier I dance with makes me think of you."

I was wrapped in a family embrace that day—unexpected by me but planned by God whose Spirit had led me to discover that stashed and forgotten box. He'd given me a most precious gift: a glimpse into my parents' hearts, their passion, and their patriotism. It has become my prize as I've grown to love my parents and my God so much more.

Lord, thank You for the myriad of wonderful ways You surprise me with Your presence. I will spend my life sharing Your faithfulness to those who call you "Father."

Jan Coleman is an author and speaker who's always looking
for "God moments." She and Carl are empty nesters.
They live in California and have a passion for travel and fishing.

An Appointment for Blessing

Debbie Alsdorf

On him we have set our hope that he will continue to deliver us.

2 Corinthians 1:10 NIV

For months it seemed I was spinning my wheels through a busy ministry schedule at our local church. I was beyond tired. As part of the pastoral staff, I was the point person when others were in need, but now my joy and energy had gone from a flame to a fizzle.

I prayed, "Father, please don't allow me to go through more than I can handle. I am in need of you."

I waited.

No answer.

Day by day, I continued on. When I prayed I heard one thing: *Trust me, I am your Deliverer.*

A woman named Kris made an appointment to see me, nothing out of the ordinary. Every week women come in who are hurting or wrapped up in terrible circumstances. I assumed Kris was another woman with a personal problem.

Entering my office with a smile as bright as sunshine, and carrying a potted miniature rose bush, she announced, "This is for you!" Setting the flowers down on my desk, she took a seat and proceeded to tell me that she had made this appointment, as led by God, to bless me and tell me how much I was loved by Him.

"You mean you made an appointment with me, just to bless me?" I asked, amazed.

"Yep! That's it." she exclaimed, smiling ear to ear.

I was speechless, knowing that she could have no idea what I had been going through. As far as anyone knew, my life was going along just fine. But, God knew—and He sent her.

We prayed together. In one moment, God's Spirit touched me, and that which had been a fizzle was once again fanned into flame. The fact that God sent unsuspecting Kris into my office showed me once again that He knows exactly what I need—and when I need it.

—ೲ—

Heavenly Father, just when I thought I couldn't make it through one more day, You touched me in a most unlikely way. I praise You for Your love and Your deliverance.

Debbie Alsdorf is the director of women's ministries at Cornerstone Fellowship in Livermore, California. She also speaks nationally and is the author of four women's Bible study books.

O Holy Night

Dolley Carlson

Every good and perfect gift is from above,
coming down from the Father.
James 1:17 NIV

No matter how old we are, our hearts always go home for
Christmas. My favorite childhood memory is Christmas Eve of
1955. It was a bare, cold New England winter; and when my
parents tucked my sister, brother, and me into our cozy beds
that night, there was no snow.

I awoke in the middle of the night and quickly went to the
window hoping to see Santa. What I saw was so much better!
While we were sleeping, heaven had covered our neighborhood
in a soft, thick blanket of snow! The moon shone in perfect
beams, the sky looked like velvet, and the silence fell upon my
ears like sacred music. Everything was snow-covered and looked
so beautiful!

Mrs. Connelly's neglected garden, covered! Mr. Ostroff's
broken roof, covered! And our black asphalt street was now a

glistening white path that looked like it could take you any-where. Thoughts of Santa vanished. Standing tippy-toe, peeking out into the night, I was so aware of the presence of God.

> *O holy night, the stars are brightly shining;*
> *It is the night of the dear Savior's birth!*
> *Long lay the world in sin and error pining,*
> *Till He appeared and the soul felt its worth.*

That night, upstairs in the house at 99 Standard Street, my little girl soul *felt its worth* because my heavenly Father was right there with me. I just knew it! Side by side, Father and beloved child, His arm and love wrapped around me for eter-nity. O Holy Night, how you blessed my little girl heart so long ago, and the blessing remains.

Remembering that Christmas Eve still brings tears to my eyes and joy to my soul.

Dearest Father, thank You for standing with me as I peer
out the many windows of life. Thank You for making
the view eternal and the blessings endless. Amen.

Dolley Carlson is an author and speaker. She has written four books, the *Gifts from the Heart* series, and traveled the globe sharing messages of hope, encouragement, inspiration, and joy.

The Man at the Door

C r i s t i n e   B o l l e y

Keep on loving each other as brothers. Do not forget
to entertain strangers, for by so doing some people
have entertained angels without knowing it.

Hebrews 13:1-2 NIV

My daughter's volleyball tournament was a good place to read in between her games. I hoped Mother Teresa's book, *In the Heart of the World*, could offer some fresh insight about the character of God.

Halfway through her stories of human encounters, she told of finding an elderly man among the Aborigines whom everyone had ignored. Mother Teresa offered to clean his dirty house, wash his clothes, and make his bed. Reluctantly, he agreed and even let her light a beautiful lamp that hadn't been lit for years. From that time, one of the sisters visited him daily. Two years later, he sent word to Teresa that the light she lit continued to shine. She said, "I thought it was a very small thing."

I wished I could encounter Jesus in people as she did.

That night we needed directions as we drove through unfamiliar neighborhoods. We pulled into a station where a scruffy, hunchbacked man in a soiled coat lingered at the front door. He seemed to be throwing something in the trash—or taking something out of it. No one wanted to walk past the man with matted hair to ask the attendant for help.

"Oh, I'll go," I said. "What can he possibly do to me with everyone watching us?" As I approached the building, he moved directly in front of the door so I couldn't avoid passing him.

And then it happened—he straightened up tall and opened the door for me to pass through. He smiled, and I watched his wrinkles disappear on his unshaven face.

"Thank you!" I said.

"It's my pleasure," he answered. I felt I had encountered the voice of God. It was a very small thing this man did for me, but the light he lit in my heart still shines.

⎯⎯⎯

Lord, forgive me for judging others. Bless my eyes so I can see people as You do. Thank You for saints who open doors that lead to knowing You better.

Cristine Bolley is an author and inspirational teacher who enjoys intimate encounters with God and loves to help others find their way home to Him, too.

Living through It

Julie Ann Barnhill

You let the distress bring you to God, not drive you from him.
The result was all gain, no loss. Distress that drives us to
God does that. It turns us around. It gets us back in the
way of salvation. We never regret that kind of pain.

2 Corinthians 7:10 THE MESSAGE

I am a woman who, ever since that tragic September eleventh morning, has wrestled with fear, anxiety, and trying to trust God. I may be a Christian believer, but absolute trust and absolute peace have often eluded me.

On October 10, 2001, I found myself in a Hollywood hotel room. Warnings of possible terrorist attacks had nearly shut down the city. A man had attempted to storm an airline cockpit, and anthrax had been discovered in yet another postal office. For the first time in my life I tasted debilitating fear. This is a fear that rapes one's sensibilities and mocks, "Abandon all hope, those who enter here."

You'd probably like to read that I prayed, read the Gideon Bible, quoted, "He has not given us the spirit of fear," and slept like a baby through the night.

Sigh. Not quite.

My encounter with God and experiencing oppressive fear that night wasn't so much about declaring victory as it was simply living through it. I was reminded of the last moments during the transition stage of childbirth: there's no going back, no way out, and your only choice is to simply live through it.

Fear drove me to God that evening, and He was there for me. I now know that none of my fears can silence the quiet, determined voice of the One who formed and cares for me.

———❦———

Lord, no matter what fears and circumstances may come
into our lives, show us how to "live through it,"
and find our peace and salvation in you.

Julie Barnhill is a national speaker and best-selling author of *She's Gonna Blow, Til Debt Do Us Part,* and *Scandalous Grace.*

An Unexpected Gift

Georgia Shaffer

Every good and perfect gift is from above,
coming down from the Father.

James 1:17 NIV

My hectic schedule forced me to lump all my shopping into the few days before Christmas. To add to my stress, several unexpected bills left little money for gifts.

One of my annual traditions is an elegant lunch followed by shopping with my Aunt Cecelia. But recent health problems had left my eighty-three-year-old aunt quite fragile. We both knew this holiday season could be her last.

The department store that day was especially chaotic because of a one-day coupon sale. The problem was I didn't have any coupons. And this became an even greater issue when I realized the price of the slacks my aunt had selected for her gift.

"Please, God, help buy these for her," I prayed. "You know my finances, and You know how much I love her." My aunt was

never one to buy clothes for herself, but she had always lavished me with lovely gifts over the years. It was important to
me that she have a special gift this year.

As we entered the dressing room to make certain the
slacks fit, I said, "Why is it I never seem to have the coupons
with me when I need them? And when I do have them, I
don't use them?"

Moments later as I knelt down to help my aunt, I heard
someone outside our dressing room door say, "I have an extra
coupon. Please take this one."

As she handed it to me, a huge burden lifted from my shoulders. Aunt Cecelia could have her slacks. This unexpected gift
from a stranger felt like it came right from the hand of God.

Father, thank You for the unexpected gifts You give
when I least expect it. Encountering You—especially
at Christmas—is the greatest gift of all.

Georgia Shaffer, speaker and producer of *The Mourning Glory Minute,*
is the author of *A Gift of Mourning Glories.*

Running Encounters with God

Carole Lewis

"Whoever has my commands and obeys them, he is the one who loves me. He who loves me will be loved by my Father, and I too will love him and show myself to him."

John 14:21 NIV

How well I remember the time that I wanted to see a co-worker lose her job. I wasn't her immediate boss, but I had influence in the department where she worked. And I fully intended to use that influence to send her packing.

One morning as I was jogging, I thought about what I was going to say to this coworker's supervisor. I was rehearsing the words in my mind, when suddenly I heard the Lord speaking to me: *Carole, do you know that I love her as much as I love you?* I was so astounded that I argued with God for almost a mile! But, by the time I reached home I had asked God to forgive me and love the woman through me.

When I arrived at the office, I immediately went down the hall to the restroom where this woman, who was always at least twenty minutes late for work, was putting on her makeup. I walked in, and after a few formalities, I asked her to forgive me if I had hurt her in any way.

To my surprise, the woman's eyes filled with tears. "Oh Carole," she said, "I thought you hated me." Soon, the tension between us was gone; and from that day on, we had a new and different relationship: one that honors Christ.

God taught me a great lesson that day. And I did my best to learn it—when I resist the urge to take matters into my own hands, and allow Him to work in the lives of others according to His speed and His wisdom, He is able to show me the worth of every individual to Him.

Father, I want to obey You today. Help me to be as loving and forgiving today as You have been to me. My prayer for today is that You would show Yourself to me.

Carole Lewis is the National Director of First Place, a Christ centered health and weight-loss program. *First Place* is used in over 12,000 churches worldwide. Adapted from "Asking Forgiveness, Gaining Peace," *Today is the First Day: Daily Encouragement on the Journey to Weight Loss and a Balanced Life,* by Carole Lewis (Ventura, CA: Gospel Light, 2002) January 10 entry.

Hooked, Netted, and Set Free

Deb Haggerty

You will again have compassion on us; you will tread our sins underfoot and hurl all our iniquities into the depths of the sea.

Micah 7:19 NIV

Minnesota is the land of 10,000 lakes (and 20,000 potholes with a fish in every one if you listen to the fishermen). It's also a land of churches. I'd grown up going to church, but I was first "hooked" when I was eighteen.

What happens when a fish is hooked? It swims up to the boat and jumps in, right? No, it struggles to get away from the hook. So did I. I swam away for years.

I had a good career. I went to church. However my private life was anything but Christian. I went through relationships like water. I drank way too much. I was so unhappy—with life and with myself.

Years later, I got married, and my husband and I began attending church. One Sunday, I heard the Lord say very strongly, *Come back to me.* I felt enveloped in love and so wanted to agree. The feeling and voice were so strong that I looked around to see if anyone else had heard.

But I thought about my past life, *Oh, no, Lord. You can't still want me. I've done too many things against Your will. I'm too bad.*

And the verse popped into my head: *All that the Father gives me will come to me, and the one who comes to me I will certainly not cast out* (John 6:37 NASB). At that moment, I was reeled in and netted. I realized that all the time I was struggling, I was still connected to His line.

Paraphrasing Micah, "The Lord takes our sins, bundles them up, then casts them into the deepest sea and posts a sign that says, No fishing!" He catches us to free us from this world, "so if the Son sets you free, you will be free indeed" (John 8:36 NIV).

Thank you, Lord, for being a patient fisherman
who always nets His catch, only to release us
into Your freedom to be with You forever.

Deb Haggerty is an author, speaker, and three-year breast cancer victor dedicated to encouraging others. She lives in Orlando, Florida with her husband, Roy, and Cocoa and Foxy the Dog.

Trouble off the Highway

Linda Evans Shepherd

I will fear no evil, for you are with me.

Psalm 23:4 NIV

When I was a college student, I drove my yellow Ford Maverick across Texas. The late afternoon sun danced through the thick pine trees lining the road. That's when I spied the Dairy Queen tucked into the forest and decided to stop for lunch.

A few minutes later, when the cashier handed me my order, I sat down in a booth in the nearly empty restaurant. To my surprise, the only other patron, a man in his thirties, slid in my booth across from me.

I looked up at him, astonished. The man, dirt smeared on his forehead, appeared to be in an alcoholic haze. He leaned in as if we were together on a date. He asked dreamily, "What are you thinking about?"

Boldly, I replied, "Do you really want to know?"

The man sat up straight. "Do I!"

"I'm thinking about Jesus," I said back with a smile.

Alarmed, the man bolted out of his chair.

"Are you one of those?" he asked.

"Of course. Is there something wrong with that?"

"N—no."

"Good," I replied. "You should think about Him too." I ate the last bite of my taco, grabbed my drink, and bolted for the door.

It took a while for the man's shock to wear off. But when it did, he rushed after me. But by that time, I was already locking my car's doors and gunning the motor. I waved goodbye with relief!

WHEW, Lord! I prayed. *Not only were You with me just now, the knowledge of Your presence kept me from potential harm. Thank You!*

I turned back onto the highway, not only grateful to be safe from a man who clearly had troubled intentions, but grateful for the Lord's presence.

———

Dear Lord, thank You for Your presence wherever I go. Help me to boldly remind others that You are near, for the knowledge of Your presence can impact a situation for good.

Linda Evans Shepherd is the founder of the *Right to the Heart of Women* online magazine and conference; both a ministry to women who minister to women and the women they serve.

About the Compilers

Linda Evans Shepherd is a nationally recognized speaker, a member of the National Speakers Association, and an award-winning, prolific author. She speaks to women who want to laugh and draw closer to God and to each other. Linda, the author of several books, including *Intimate Moments with God*, has been on countless radio and TV programs from coast to coast. In addition, Linda founded a new ministry for women who minister to women called Right to the Heart of Women (www.righttotheheartof-women.com), as well as the Advanced Writers and Speakers Association (www.awsawomen.com) and a national radio program, *Right to the Heart* (www.righttotheheart.com).

Married for more than twenty years, Linda has two children and is President of Shepherd Heart Productions (www.sheppro.com).

⸙

Eva Marie Everson is a nationally recognized speaker and the 2002 AWSA Member of the Year. She has authored several books, including a suspense/intrigue trilogy: *Shadow of Dreams*, *Summon the Shadows*, and *Shadows of Light*.

In the summer of 2002, Eva Marie traveled with five other Christian journalists to Israel for a special ten-day press trip that, in turn, changed her life. Upon her return, she authored the highly acclaimed "Falling Into the Bible" series for Crosswalk.com and enrolled in seminary.

Married to Dennis, Eva Marie has four children and three grandchildren. The goal of her ministry is to draw others into a more intimate relationship with God. Eva Marie's website can be found at www.evamarieeverson.com.

About the Advanced Writers and Speakers Association (AWSA)

Advanced Writers and Speakers Association is a professional support group made up of the top 10 percent of Christian women in both publishing and speaking. Currently, we are more than two hundred women strong and are sponsored by the 501 (c) 3 nonprofit ministry of Right to the Heart.

Our main event is the annual AWSA conference which is held just prior to the opening of the CBA (Christian Booksellers') Trade Show. We also sponsor prayer teleconferences, prayer retreats, and the Golden Scroll Awards Banquet.

Our communication centers around an online loop where we find connection and prayer support with those who are traveling similar journeys. Our members can choose to be contacted daily or only for special announcements.

Our Golden Scroll Awards Banquet also takes place just prior to the opening of CBA. We invite authors, editors, and publishers to gather for our presentation of the Golden Scroll Member, Editor, and Publisher of the Year Awards.

We are open to those Christian women communicators who have published at least two books and who speak to groups of one hundred at least three times a year across state lines. To join AWSA, fill out our online membership application at the following website:

www.awsawomen.com

For more information on how you can personally encounter God, go to:

www.encounterswithgod.com

Additional copies of this book are available
from your local bookstore.

Also look for:

Intimate Moments with God

If you have enjoyed this book, or if it has impacted your life,
we would like to hear from you.

Please contact us at:

Honor Books
An Imprint of Cook Communications Ministries
4050 Lee Vance View
Colorado Springs, CO 80918

www.cookministries.com